How to Get the Best out of your man

D0110618

How to Get the Best

out of your

man

michelle mckinney hammond

HARVEST HOUSE PUBLISHERS
EUGENE, OREGON

Unless otherwise indicated, all Scripture quotations are taken from The ESV® Bible (The Holy Bible, English Standard Version®), copyright © 2001 by Crossway, a publishing ministry of Good News Publishers. Used by permission. All rights reserved.

Verses marked NLT are taken from the Holy Bible, New Living Translation, copyright © 1996, 2004, 2007 by Tyndale House Foundation. Used by permission of Tyndale House Publishers, Inc., Carol Stream, Illinois 60188. All rights reserved.

Verses marked NIV are taken from the Holy Bible, New International Version® NIV®. Copyright © 1973, 1978, 1984, 2011 by Biblica, Inc.™ Used by permission of Zondervan. All rights reserved worldwide. www.zondervan.com

Verses marked NKJV are taken from the New King James Version. Copyright © 1982 by Thomas Nelson, Inc. Used by permission. All rights reserved.

Verses marked TLB are taken from The Living Bible, Copyright © 1971. Used by permission of Tyndale House Publishers, Inc., Wheaton, IL 60189 USA. All rights reserved.

Verses marked MSG are taken from The Message. Copyright © by Eugene H. Peterson 1993, 1994, 1995, 1996, 2000, 2001, 2002. Used by permission of NavPress Publishing Group.

Verses marked GNT are taken from the Good News Translation—Second Edition © 1992 by American Bible Society. Used by permission.

Cover illustration © liquidlibrary/Thinkstock

Cover design by Koechel Peterson & Associates Inc., Minneapolis, Minnesota

Michelle McKinney Hammond is represented by the literary agency of Alive Communications, Inc., 7680 Goddard Street, Ste. 200, Colorado Springs, CO 80920. www.alivecommunications.com

HOW TO GET THE BEST OUT OF YOUR MAN
Copyright © 2013 by Michelle McKinney Hammond
Published by Harvest House Publishers
Eugene, Oregon 97402
www.harvesthousepublishers.com

Library of Congress Cataloging-in-Publication Data
McKinney Hammond, Michelle.
    How to get the best out of your man / Michelle McKinney Hammond.
        pages cm
    ISBN 978-0-7369-3790-0 (pbk.)
    ISBN 978-0-7369-4266-9 (eBook)
    1. Single women—Religious life. 2. Christian women—Religious life. 3. Man–woman relationships—Biblical teaching. 4. Man–woman relationships—Religious aspects—Christianity. 5. Bible. O.T. Esther—Criticism, interpretation, etc. I. Title.
    BV4596.S5M3447 2013
    248.8'435—dc23

                                                                        2012036122

All rights reserved. No part of this publication may be reproduced, stored in a retrieval system, or transmitted in any form or by any means—electronic, mechanical, digital, photocopy, recording, or any other—except for brief quotations in printed reviews, without the prior permission of the publisher.

Printed in the United States of America

13 14 15 16 17 18 19 20 / BP-JH / 10 9 8 7 6 5 4 3 2 1

To every woman who has a heart for God and for her man—
may you be reassured there is power in doing things God's way.

To my long-term examples that God's principles are not only true but
workable...

> ❧ *William and Norma McKinney—what wonderful parents*
> *you have been! What a solid example of love and marriage you*
> *have shown me over the years. You set the bar high and proved*
> *it's possible to have an amazing friendship and marriage with*
> *the partner of your dreams.*

> ❧ *Frank and Bunny Wilson—your marriage has always been a*
> *beacon of light to countless others and an oasis of sweet reassur-*
> *ance for me. Frank, you are sorely missed, but you left a legacy*
> *of love behind for us to treasure.*

> ❧ *To all the others—you know who you are! Watching you*
> *do love and marriage has been a pleasure as well as a con-*
> *firmation that marriage can be a happy place and a real*
> *partnership.*

CENTRAL ARKANSAS LIBRARY SYSTEM
SIDNEY S. McMATH BRANCH LIBRARY
LITTLE ROCK, ARKANSAS

Acknowledgments

To my Harvest House family. One thing about a good house is no matter what the weather in our lives, the house is still standing. So happy to be in the family after all these years, looking forward to many more.

To Barb, my trusty editor, thank you for hanging in there with me through all my various transitions. You remain the voice of reason ☺.

To Dave Koechel, thanks for making my babies look pretty on the shelves.

To all those who work tirelessly to help me get the word out, "Thank you!"

Contents

Part 1

Who Is He?

hen you look at your man, who do you see? The real man or the man you would like to see? Somewhere between a wonderful combination of both lies the true man, with all his hopes, fears, accomplishments, and disappointments. The man God created him to be, the man you hoped for, and the man he longs to be converge in different degrees in response to circumstances, stresses (real or imagined), love, rejection, fulfillment, and the search for what confirms his identity as a man. These things will affect his responses to you and the world at large on any given day.

It's been said that men are far less complex than women, and I believe that is true. When women understand the basics about men, we'll find it much easier to relate to them.

In the Beginning...

In the Bible, the first time man is mentioned has him in a remote place being fashioned by God. No wonder so many men think they are God's gift to the world. They literally are. And later, God created woman for man, which makes us God's gift to them.

God created man in His own likeness. This creative move on God's part is our first telling hint for solving the mystery of a man's heart. If he is made in the image of God, then we must know that he will imitate God in unending ways, including emotionally and spiritually. He will be driven to reflect his maker from the core of his soul because he is an extension of the God who created him. (Yes, the same is true for women, but we are focusing on men in this book.)

God craves relationship, honor, worship, and victory—the same things a man craves. As we move through this book, we'll break these things down and deal with them one by one.

For now, keep in mind that God created us all for relationship. He doesn't need anyone other than Himself, yet He desires fellowship and a love relationship with us. He wants to know that He is appreciated and honored for all He has done and does for us. He delights in all His creation working well together and seeing His will accomplished in our lives. The ultimate tribute to His Lordship is the victory that is experienced when we submit totally to Him, forsaking all other influences and temptations.

Does that sound familiar? It sounds like all of us—including your man! We will be taking an in-depth look at what this looks like in our relationships as we move forward, but suffice it to say that a man looks to his woman to provide a lot of those good feelings. The rewards for fulfilling his desires can be above and beyond what we can even imagine.

When God created woman, she was fashioned to meet the needs of her man. You see, God made man with a very specific assignment in mind. He was created not just for fellowship but also to supervise and manage God's creation. He was created to be fruitful, to multiply, to subdue and have dominion over all that God had made. Small wonder man is driven to conquer in every area of his world. This stuff is in his genes by divine design. But guess what? He is only able to accomplish these things partially unless he has the help of a woman (and God, of course). Both man and woman were commanded to be fruitful, multiply, take dominion over every living thing and subdue evil, but this work would require a partnership between the man and the woman. These commands could not be accomplished alone. In this book, we will be focusing on the man as we move forward so we can better understand our men and their needs.

I've said it before, and I'll say it again: Man is the *starter*, but woman is the *finisher*. She is the period at the end of his sentence. She brings completion to his world, along with a healthy dose of the support it takes for him to accomplish his tasks. In Africa one saying goes, "Man is the head, woman is the neck. Wherever the neck turns, the head turns." Yes, it's true. God has given woman an amazing gift that can be more powerful than a man's authority. It is the *gift of influence*. When utilized well, everyone in that couple's world benefits from the fruit of their harmonious union. Couples that operate according to God's design positively impact and stabilize their world. The effects of what happens within their relationship can progressively improve relations and conditions in their neighborhood, community, and nation.

In every relationship—our relationship with God, our relationship with our man, our relationship with others—there are principles and protocols that help us achieve the results we want. As we bless God, He blesses us. When we bring pleasure to His heart, He goes out of His way to pour divine surprises from heaven into ours. He crowns us with His favor and opens doors that can't be shut before us. The same is true of man. A happy husband makes a happy wife.

As we focus on how to get the best out of your mate and your relationship, I will be sharing principles that were utilized by a very famous woman back in biblical times. Queen Esther's life, detailed in the book of Esther, conveys principles that are still profound and powerful for our modern-day lives. Blending femininity with wisdom is a force that will always bear wonderful results. Though God has given women tremendous sensitivity, an uncanny sense of discernment, and inherent wisdom in many areas, it is not *what* we say sometimes but *how* we say it that makes the difference. It's not always what we *do,* but *when* and *how* we do it that can make or break our relationships.

The principles I'm about to share with you work across the board, not just on spouses. They will be effective in our workplaces, with friends, and even with strangers. The values and behaviors that invite the participation of God and His favor into our everyday situations cannot be compartmentalized. The Bible tells us that Jesus gained favor with God and man. This fact reveals that as we align ourselves with the Word of God, doing things God's way, not only do we gain favor by giving Him pleasure, it has the trickle-down effect of creating favor with everyone we encounter. God can even cause our enemies to be at peace with us.

This is a fine position to be in when we're ready to negotiate with our mates for something that is important to us. Most positive outcomes begin with favor being present. The blessing of a positive attitude or atmosphere provides an open door to achieving what we want in life, from an enhanced love relationship to a job, from peace in our homes to rich friendships and encounters that yield lasting fruit.

Now you might be thinking, "Michelle, I don't aspire to get the best out of my man. I would be happy with just the basics." Rest assured, the same principles apply. Unfortunately, relationships are one of the few careers that no one studies for yet we all expect to be successful in them. Maybe we think we'll be good at them through osmosis. As if just because relationships are all around us, we'll just naturally be good at them. Unfortunately, that just doesn't happen.

There are things we do as women that will inspire men to fly, and other things we do that can cause them to crash and want to abdicate their posts in our lives. Hopefully as we unpack the principles found in the book of Esther, we will put into practice some principles that will garner positive results and improve our relationships with our men specifically, as well as people in general. We should never demand or require what we want. Even when that's effective in the short-term, it generates negativity and seldom lasts. Instead, we should be influencers who inspire the right response from others.

That being said, this is *not* a manual on how to manipulate our men. *How to Get the Best Out of Your Man* is a guide to being the kind of woman who *inspires* her man to rise to the occasion and be the man God created him to be—a man who loves you as Christ loves you and gave Himself for you.

The true expression of love is selfless giving to the very point of laying down your life for the person you love. This goes both ways for both partners.

As we approach everyday life, as well as the emergencies and unique issues life throws our way, our responses and the manner in which we interact with others will determine the outcome. Some of the principles and actions I'm going to share may go against the grain of popular thought and today's attitudes, but they are time-tested values and standards that have endured and worked for generation after generation. Keep in mind that no matter how times change, the human spirit remains rooted in God's original design. He has wired men and women to very specific roles, and life works best for us when we consult and live by God's blueprint. Just as you cannot drive a computer or create data with a car, all things created need to function according to their design if they are to work at their optimum levels and accomplish their purpose.

Men and women are different. "No kidding!" you say. For a while the focus was on the many ways men and women are alike to help eliminate disparities in jobs, wages, and a host of other issues. But now we can look at the differences, and they are good! Men and women bring different sets of strengths and weaknesses to the party. This means that between the two sexes life can be balanced beautifully if the two parties honor and respect those differences. Life will get truly exciting the more we discover how to create and support that balance.

Are you ready to get started? I certainly am. Let's take a journey to ancient Persia to discover the amazing ways one woman influenced her man and how that affected an entire nation. Let's glean from her life enduring relationship principles that will enhance our own lives and relationships. Then we can be a positive force in the lives of our men… and everyone else we interact with.

1

Male by Design

In those days when King Ahasuerus sat on his royal throne in Susa, the capital, in the third year of his reign he gave a feast for all his officials and servants. The army of Persia and Media and the nobles and governors of the provinces were before him, while he showed the riches of his royal glory and the splendor and pomp of his greatness for many days, 180 days (Esther 1:2-5).

King Ahasuerus (also called King Xerxes) knew how to celebrate! His was the party to end all parties. Celebrity fests in Hollywood had nothing on this gathering—six months of revelry in sheer opulence to celebrate himself. He was the man of the hour seated on his throne to watch the celebration unfold before him. Yes, the king was in his glory. His dominion stretched from India to Ethiopia, but even now he was planning his next conquest.

In the meantime, he'd invited all those who served him to come and get a taste of what he was used to on an everyday basis. His excess could be theirs only for a short time, but for now they were drunk—inebriated not only from the wine but also their surroundings. The king's lordship was evident. No one could live like this except a great king. From the glistening marble floors to the rich tapestries, from the golden vessels and utensils to the delectable food—everything bespoke the mighty person in whose presence they had the good fortune to find themselves. It was a heady experience to have this up-close access to such power and wealth.

Susa was the king's slice of heaven on earth, a place set high above most of his domain and surrounded by a fortress that contained the splendor of his worldly acquisitions. King Ahasuerus surrounded himself with the finest of the fine. Nothing was out of his reach. And for six months now, he'd granted to all of his subjects access to him and a glimpse of what it was like to be king. Now the people were invested. Now they felt they were truly part of the kingdom. Now they would defend it as never before. Yes, the celebration was accomplishing what the king desired. His subjects saw him as he truly was—powerful, generous, and great.

He wanted their allegiance, their reverence, their awe. He bathed in the honor they gave him. It unleashed his desire to reach out even more. So he extended the party for another seven days and allowed his citizens to even enjoy his personal garden. It was here they experienced pleasures beyond their imagination. Wine flowed liberally and was theirs for the asking. They could partake as much as they wanted. Nothing was off limits. Nothing had to be purchased.

I'm sure the people said, "This king is so generous!" and "What an amazing king we have!" Every act of kindness brought the king more praise, which heightened his desire to share more of himself and all he possessed. Amid the celebration, King Ahasuerus sat back and took in the crowd around him. *This is the life. To conquer, to rule, to be honored.* He found it interesting to people watch. Each person was different and unique. No two looked alike—much like the goblets he served wine in. He prided himself on possessing the best, the one-of-a-kind items. Each cup was cast with a unique design so not one of them was like another. His people were here together, and he was lord over them all! He lifted a glass in response to their toast and drank deep. *Yes, this is the life!*

〜♾️〜

In the man Adam, God essentially created a being patterned after Himself. Adam (and all men after him) was a living soul clothed in a body with a spirit that modeled many of the qualities and desires of his creator. Therefore, man has a "kingdom mentality." He is wired to be lord of his sphere of influence, his space, his profession, his home, and, yes, even his woman. Although woman was given the same authority and dominion, God holds the man responsible for the woman's well being.

A famous disc jockey on a morning talk show would always say, "I got the gift, and I've got to use it!" This is so true of men. They can't help themselves! They have to be fruitful, to be productive. They have to multiply—to extend their sphere of influence. They want to have dominion—to rule their space and be significantly in charge. They want to subdue anything that challenges their power or threatens the safety of those they love.

Oh yes, man was created to be lord over his domain. God placed the first man in the Garden of Eden and then commanded him to be and do all I just mentioned. This was a *God-given* directive, not a self-inspired realization. God deliberately wired man this way to show us His attributes and help us better understand His heart. Man was divinely created male by design. When a man is surrendered to God, his character reflects who God is. This is how God is glorified. And as a man loves his woman the way Christ loved the church and gave Himself for it, we again see the character and heart of God at work right before our very eyes.

In the world today the lines of sexuality are blurred. Many people are quick to take offense at what are actually the natural inclinations of both sexes. Men are wired to conquer, to fix things, to lead. This doesn't mean women are relegated to a weaker status or a less-than role, although physically we aren't built to sustain what men can in their bodies.

When I read the creation story, I see that God has a special place in His heart for women. The fact that He would create men and then hold them accountable for the care of women and all that He created makes a huge statement. God expects men to live up to the mandate of every one of His charges given that day in the garden. This is why Adam suffered such severe consequences when he didn't cover Eve and protect her from the wiles of the serpent. Instead, Adam followed her lead and sinned against God.

"Because you listened to your wife…cursed is the ground because of you," God said (Genesis 3:17). Adam abdicated his post. He left his woman exposed. No one who understands the worth of what he has exposes anything he considers precious to danger. The fact that God would encourage husbands to care for their wives properly lest the men have their prayers hindered suggests that women are precious to God and held in His high esteem (1 Peter 3:7).

But let's get back to the men (we'll cover women later). The bottom line is we shouldn't get upset when our men want to lead. They have been created to do so—even *commanded* to do so for our sake. If we women can see men taking their rightful positions as leaders as a positive, the war between the sexes would be won.

How does this principle manifest? We need to view our homes and surrounding areas as mini kingdoms. A man wants to be a significant part of his surroundings. He is driven to make his mark. Men must make their mark on their world that announces to everyone, "I was here! I am an important contributor to what you have witnessed."

How does this relate to us? What impact does this drive have on our relationship with our men? Trust me on this: If a man doesn't feel significant in his home, if he doesn't feel as if he reigns in his personal world, he will find somewhere else to rule. Whether it's at work, an extracurricular activity, the arms of another woman…he will most definitely find a niche to be lord over. Man was made to be king of his personal domain, to "hold it down," as some people say.

Your man's identity as a man is wrapped up in what he is able to produce and how much in control he is. I find it interesting that even though no woman wants to feel as if she is being controlled or beneath her man, how quickly she will become disappointed or lose respect if her man appears weak, out of control, or not on top of the situation. If he doesn't appear to be leading, his mate—his woman—often gets impatient and wonders why she must be the one to take the lead or come up with ideas and solutions for a given situation.

Deep in her core, a woman's spirit recognizes a man who is or is not operating according to God's design. And as we women and our partners drive in our own lanes, following the ways God designed us, we will find our relationships moving forward in an orderly fashion with a lot fewer collisions. This is when the relationship journey becomes beautiful, harmonious, and fruitful. Perhaps this is why we strive to better understand our mates. Understanding each other is key to having a vibrant, successful relationship that makes life a slice of heaven on earth.

Reflections

❧ What modern-day deceptions do you grapple with when it comes to the traditional roles of men and women in relationships?

❧ Consider your mate or significant male figure in your life. In what ways does he reflect God's design for man?

❧ In what ways do you celebrate those traits in him?

❧ In what ways do you help him be significant and make his mark?

Love Talk

As we respect and honor our God-given designs, temperaments, and personalities, we will have richer unions that are visible celebrations of the goodness and love of God. These attributes will attract others to God and His kingdom.

2

What a Man Wants

*Drinks were served in gold goblets of many designs, and there was
an abundance of royal wine, reflecting the king's generosity. By
edict of the king, no limits were placed on the drinking, for the king
had instructed all his palace officials to serve each man as much
as he wanted. At the same time, Queen Vashti gave a banquet for
the women in the royal palace of King Xerxes (Esther 1:7-9 NLT).*

King Ahasuerus, also known as King Xerxes, gazed in pleasure at
the delight of his subjects. Nothing pleased him more than being
the source of joy and revelry for his citizens. To be able to display his
generosity in such unlimited measure was sure to impress. What other
person had the resources to be so liberal? Not only did the king possess
a vast supply of the best wines, he obviously could afford to give them
away freely. He spared no expense for this celebration. From the best
wines to the golden vessels they were poured into, he withheld nothing.

From his nobles and officials, to the princes of his provinces, to the
citizens surrounding his citadel, he extended the invitation to all to
come, drink, and be merry. No one was forced to drink, but they were
given permission to partake as much as they pleased. And the people
did! They experienced the king's goodness and provision.

The king took delight in providing for his people. This was what he lived for. This was the confirmation of who he was. This moment spoke to the core of his soul. It reaffirmed who he was—a man, a real man. No, he was more than that. He was king. He was large and in charge. He was in control of his own space and his domain. He was a conqueror, reigning supreme. His position in life was clear and could not be questioned. He was secure in who he was and what he accomplished.

King Ahasuerus leaned back. The only thing missing was his woman…his beautiful queen. He knew she was hosting the women while the revelry continued around him, but he longed for her presence. He wondered how her party was progressing. He pictured her surrounded by other women admiring her—her beauty and her position. She was exquisite, and she belonged to him. No one else could lay claim to her attention and affection.

As the music swirled around the king, the voices of the people became muted. He was transported in thought to a quieter, more intimate moment with his queen. She was so beautiful! So soft to the touch…so warm…so loving. He loved the way he felt when he was in her company. It was the only time he could truly be himself. Where he could drop all the posturing and pretense. He could be just a man wrapped in the arms of his woman…touching her, loving her, and being loved in return. He could whisper secrets to her and know they would remain hidden in her heart.

Ah, yes, Vashti was something else. A work of art. A treasure that belonged to him. But right now she was about the business of being queen. She was hosting a party of her own. He loved her independence. He'd made the right choice in choosing her. She was able to stand beside him but also able to stand alone. She was not a clinging vine, and yet she knew when to cling to him. She released him to take care of business, but she also knew how to be the most welcome and delightful distraction in his world.

The more King Ahasuerus thought about Vashti, the more he missed her. It had been a while. He'd been overwhelmed with the affairs of state and entertaining—the responsibilities and duties a man must do as king. Perhaps they had been apart too long. Well, he knew how to fix that. The sounds of the room assaulted him as his reverie was broken, bringing him back to the present. He turned to look for his eunuchs. Catching the gaze of one, he lifted his hand in summons.

Every man must be a master. It is a confirmation of who he is as a man. He longs to be a leader, a provider, a husband, a father. He lives to be the source of everything his loved ones need. And when he isn't, he struggles with a tremendous sense of failure.

The first basic need all humans have, whether male or female, is that of being significant. After that they need variety, they need to be loved, they need to grow, and they need to make a contribution to the world—a legacy, if you will, that remains after they leave this earth.

The stress and expectation of attaining these needs doesn't weigh as heavily on a woman as it does a man. To a man, his failure to live up to the expectations of what men do—succeed at a career, be a leader, protect and provide for the family, and be in control of a host of circumstances—makes him question who is he. His masculinity is on the line. As Jezebel demanded of King Ahab when he was sulking in his bed over a vineyard he wanted and couldn't get, "Are you the king of Israel or not?" (1 Kings 21:7 NLT). Now perhaps today's woman isn't expecting her man to be a king, but she is expecting him to be a man. When he falls down on his job or responsibilities, she asks him the same question, whether it be silently through her attitude, via a disparaging look, or spoken: "Are you a man or not?"

A man dreads this confrontation. Everything within him longs to be *the* man in his woman's eyes. Though he may not express it, no one feels his failure more deeply than he does. When challenged by his woman, he will abdicate rather than fight if he is a man. In the face of constant criticism and belittling, boys fight and men walk away or redirect to other sources where they can earn respect, admiration, and praise.

A man wants his woman to be able to depend on him without being paralyzed herself. He wants to be her hero but not her oxygen. There is a balance in this thing called relationships. A man wants his woman to be his oasis, but not drain him with her neediness. He wants to be able to trust his heart and the deep issues of his life to her without fearing exposure or ridicule. He doesn't want to be taken advantage of or used, although he dreams of providing for all her needs. Solomon's mother, Bathsheba, brings up this point as she is instructing him in what to look for in a wife: "The heart of her husband safely trusts in her…She does him good not evil all the days of her life" (Proverbs 31:11-12 NKJV).

A woman has everything to do with how a man feels about himself. She can make or break his universe. She can shatter him with one look and inspire him to greatness with another. She can be the greatest influence in his life. Therefore, she should use her influence well. Remember, it was Eve who influenced Adam to eat of the forbidden fruit in the Garden of Eden. If you ever feel powerless, simply remember that event in the history of mankind that affected us all—and all because of the influence of a woman. This is what Solomon's mother knew and was trying to convey as she advised him on the type of woman who would be beneficial to his life.

A man wants a sister, friend, partner, lover. Notice I omitted the word "mother." He already has one. He wants a woman who will be a "helpmeet" for him. A woman who is a complement to him, who brings strengths to the relationship that he doesn't possess. She is a help to him, someone who will work with him not against him. A woman who will be one with him but also have an identity of her own. A woman who brings her own special brand of who she is as an asset to her man. If you recall, Queen Vashti held her own celebration during King Ahasuerus's lavish celebration. She hosted her own party in her own chambers, leaving her man to do what he does.

Despite his need to be needed, the burden to be his woman's everything is too much for any man to carry. Nor was he designed to. God will not share His glory with another. If your man was your everything, you would have no need of God—and God will never allow that. So He allows sin to do what it does in our lives. It causes us to fail one another from time to time, reminding us of our need for a flawless God. A true woman has a life enriched by her man but not wholly dependent on her man. And that is what every man wants.

Reflections

✻ Who are you apart from your man?

✻ In what ways do you contribute positively to your man?

✻ What do you do to inspire trust in your man?

Love Talk

One of the greatest gifts you can give your man is room enough so that he can be who he is.

3

What a Man Needs

On the seventh day of the feast, when King Xerxes was in high
spirits because of the wine, he told the seven eunuchs who attended
him…to bring Queen Vashti to him with the royal crown on her
head. He wanted the nobles and all the other men to gaze on her
beauty, for she was a very beautiful woman (Esther 1:10-11 NLT).

King Xerxes [Ahasuerus] thought it was well and good that his queen wasn't one to nag, crowd his space, or seek his constant attention. All his women weren't that way. If left to their own devices, they would forever be in his presence, barraging him with their concerns real or imagined. This could interrupt affairs of state if left unchecked, and he would forever be distracted from matters that were more urgent—affairs of the kingdom that might threaten the security of his reign and his people. He needed to be able to focus. His kingdom was his first priority because far too many people depended on him. For this reason, he'd set strict boundaries for his household, including his wives and concubines. One rule was that they were not allowed to come into his presence or approach him without being summoned by him.

But Vashti…she was different. She was her own woman even though she was his. She was the epitome of the meaning of her name: "desired, beloved." She was secure in who she was. Ahasuerus might be the king, but she was definitely the queen. And she knew it. She embodied and embraced her position fully. Ahasuerus chuckled as he thought about her strong will and some of the things she said. Lesser men would have been threatened by her, but he was not. He found her intriguing…stimulating, in fact. She was a pleasant diversion from all the "yes" men who cowered in his presence or simply went along with anything he said because of his position. The king looked forward to exchanges with Vashti. He never knew what to expect, and this always left him wanting more of her. She was a treasure chest of pleasant surprises, and he couldn't wait for the next one.

The more he thought of her, the more he missed her. His eyes scanned the room. He'd been surrounded by men long enough. He would send for her. Yes, that's what he would do. If his guests thought the splendor of his palace was a thing to behold, just wait until they saw his wife! She was a true work of art and exquisite in her beauty. She was the finest thing he'd acquired to date.

He hesitated only briefly as he thought of the law that women were not to show themselves in public. But he was king! He created the law. The wine in his system urged him past his reservations. He could do as he pleased, even if that meant breaking his own laws. He wanted to see her, and he wanted to see her now.

On that note he got the attention of his eunuchs, who served him continually. He dispatched them with a note to the queen. Now all he had to do was sit back and wait. She would be here soon, and all would gaze with great appreciation at her beauty. He didn't consider her a "trophy" wife—or at least he would never admit to that. He would say she had the right combination of beauty and smarts. She was not only beautiful, but she also had social graces that were unrivaled. She was a force to be reckoned with. He found her engaging and entertaining. Oh yes, once she arrived, the room would be filled with electricity. This he knew; this he anticipated. And at the end of the day the pleasure would be all his.

Many have said that men are intimidated by successful women, but most of the men I interviewed denied this. Perhaps I need to emphasize that I am talking about men—not boys. Men who are secure in their identity as men. As our conversations evolved on the topic of strong, independent, successful women, the bottom line from the men became clear. Most men wanted a woman they wouldn't have to worry about should anything happen to them. They didn't want a helpless woman who wouldn't be able to take care of herself and their family. They liked the idea of being able to brag about the achievements of their wives. However, this is where the conversation also veered to what makes a successful woman unpleasant (but not intimidating). For instance, when a woman celebrated herself and her achievements more than she celebrated her man and what he shared, that was a negative. Or when she kept constantly reminding him of what she'd achieved without his help. Opera singer syndrome, you know, always singing "me, me, me," saying I did this or I got that was found to be very unattractive.

Now, before you get your neck all twisted up, ready to hurl accusations of sexism, think about it this way. Let's flip the script. What if you were with a man who constantly let you know he didn't really need you? He did well all on his own. What if you were married to him, and he went off and bought houses and cars without sharing the experiences with you? What if your "partner" didn't act like a team player, all in the name of being strong and independent? That kind of defeats the purpose of being in relationship, doesn't it? In light of the fact that we all need to feel significant, especially in the lives of our loved ones, what would that do to our morale?

So it's safe to say that a man's concerns about overly "self-sufficient" women can be warranted at times. What this tells us, is that we need to find the best balance in celebrating our accomplishments without letting them define or overtake our identities. At the end of the day, we are not what we *do*, we are who we *are*. Out of our *being* comes all the things we *do*.

God is the great "I Am." He simply is. Out of His being flows all of His attributes. He is not defined by what He does, He is defined by who He is. In the same way, a woman is defined in God's eyes by who she is inherently. The world pushes us to be defined by what we do, what we own, who we know—all things that don't last. This is dangerous because if we lose these things, we may believe we lose ourselves, our identity. Do we really? Absolutely not! We are still who we are.

A man wants to celebrate his woman. Yes, he wants to put you on display, with the major emphasis being what a great *woman* you are. You are his woman, his greatest acquisition. Not in the sense that you are a trophy or an inanimate object, but from the viewpoint that someone as great as you chose him above all others. This is the best proof that you saw something great in him. And this heightens his feeling of significance. It boosts him as a man and makes him want to strive to be greater. Why? Because in his mind you expect it.

The fact that you have interests outside of him is great because it releases him from being completely responsible for your fulfillment. When you make a man feel he is your everything, that makes him nervous. It's too much pressure. What if he fails or doesn't live up to your expectations? He wants you to have other interests, to have strengths of your own, to, in a sense, throw your own party while he is throwing his. But he also wants you to know when it's the right time to come together and make it totally about each other with none of those outside influences intruding on your personal and intimate space.

A woman needs to know when to leave her work and all that she does behind and enter into the secret place with her man, when he can feel that he is her everything. He is her king, and she is his queen. That's how great kingdoms are built.

Reflections

❧ In what ways do you battle finding the best balance between who you are and what you do?

❧ What really defines you as a woman?

❧ In what ways do you make your man feel significant?

Love Talk

In relationships, it's not about who you are. It's about how you make the other person feel. This is the first law of selflessness. Until we are willing to empty ourselves for another—and then do it—we will not experience complete fulfillment in any relationship.

4

The Problem with Submission

Queen Vashti refused to come at the king's command delivered by the eunuchs. At this the king became enraged, and his anger burned within him... Then Memucan said in the presence of the king and the officials, "Not only against the king has Queen Vashti done wrong, but also against all the officials and all the peoples who are in all the provinces of King Ahasuerus. For the queen's behavior will be made known to all women, causing them to look at their husbands with contempt" (Esther 1:12,16-17).

The king saw his servants returning from the mission to bring the queen, but where was Vashti? He sensed something wasn't right. "Where is the queen?" he asked.

The eunuchs glanced at one another, shifting their weight uncomfortably. Each waited for the other to speak up. The longer the pause, the greater the king's impatience became. He'd sent them on a simple errand—to convey a note requesting the presence of his queen. A great amount of time had passed, and he'd assumed they were waiting for her to get ready to accompany them to the throne room. Now the servants had arrived with no queen.

"Where is she?" The question rang in his mind, causing him to repeat it a bit too loudly. The room quieted around him as tension filled the air. It was apparent to everyone in attendance that the king wasn't pleased.

Finally Memucan inched forward to deliver the bad news. The queen had refused to come...

"What? The queen refuses to come?" His voice filled the air and echoed in the great hall. Would Vashti dare to disgrace him in front of his peers? Was he king or not? Had he not requested her presence? Was she to overlook his desires and usurp his authority? She was insulting him publicly!

All the pleasure of the festivities, the wine, and even those in his presence celebrating him faded. Anger replaced good spirits and was accompanied by a hearty dose of offense. How dare she! His eyes bore holes into the eunuchs who stood before him, causing them to shift uneasily again, not knowing what to expect next. In anger and frustration he waved them away, while searching the room for his advisers.

Locating them huddled together, he beckoned them forward. Slowly they came as he motioned them to move forward more quickly. They quickened their pace, arriving before the king and his anger with great apprehension. He searched their faces to see what they thought about this horrible situation. Finally he asked, "What is to be done to Queen Vashti, because she has not performed the command of King Ahasuerus?" In the heat of emotion, he didn't stop to think what this question asked in public might cost him. He had to save face. He had to regain his authority. He couldn't be publicly disgraced by a woman... his wife...his queen without issuing a consequence. He would be seen in the wrong light and unable to rule his kingdom effectively if even one seed of disrespect was allowed to grow unchecked.

His noblemen seconded his fears that were voiced by Memucan. If the queen were allowed to get away with this total disregard for the authority of the king, her behavior would spread like yeast throughout the kingdom. Other women would disrespect their husbands as well. Chaos would reign throughout the kingdom if such a blatant show of rebellion were permitted to pass without sanction. The king was worried about his kingdom, and his wise men were worried about their personal kingdoms.

One woman held enough power to create anarchy in every household in the kingdom. After all, Queen Vashti was a role model, a public figure. Her marriage and conduct were on display. She had the power to sway the mindset of society. She must be dealt with severely so that all who were subject to the king would remain in their rightful places. Defiance could not be tolerated. By popular vote and a wave of the hand, Queen Vashti's fate was sealed. She was to be banned from the kingdom so the memory of her refusal would be silenced forevermore.

~~~

"Submission." A small word that creates huge controversy. Perhaps because it hasn't been thought through thoroughly. In thinking about Queen Vashti, several possible scenarios run through my mind. The first one? Perhaps Vashti wasn't so pleased to have to throw a party and entertain womenfolk for more than six months. And maybe she was unhappy that such a long time had passed before her husband decided he wanted to see her. Her obstinate refusal might have been her way of venting her displeasure.

To this scenario, I respond, "Never answer anyone when you're angry or fearful about a situation." In the heat of the moment, you will probably answer or act wrongly. One of the issues women of successful men have always struggled with is the lack of time available to spend with their men. Ironic, isn't it, that some women want wealthy, powerful men, but they forget those men will be busy pursuing wealth or wielding their influence. After all, that's usually how they became wealthy and powerful. They work harder than the average Joe.

If you're dealing with this kind of man, you must be able to entertain yourself and know that having to wait now will be worth it later in life. Men of means lead seasonal lives—seedtime and harvest. Many a woman departs before the harvest, thus leaving her rewards to another woman who didn't have to wait through the time of planting and weeding. You deserve the reward, so be patient and wait for it.

A second scenario entertains the possibility that Vashti's refusal to go to the king wasn't that deep or that big of a deal. She knew the king had decreed that women were not to show themselves in public in the manner he was now asking her to. Though she was flattered that he wanted to display her beauty, she also knew she would be breaking his law. She knew he had been drinking quite a bit, and perhaps he was making a bad decision in the midst of being inebriated. Maybe she thought the king would sleep off his wine overindulgence and forget about everything in the morning. Maybe she figured he was drunk so why heed his request and be made of fool of?

Let's say that for whatever reason, Vashti's refusal was legitimate and reasonable. That she was right not to respond to the king's request to come show herself. There have been countless arguments and speculations about her reasoning throughout the ages. The bottom line is that sometimes when we choose to stand on principle, we end up standing alone. We have to weigh the cost to see if the price of being right is worth losing the entire relationship.

Or perhaps there was a better way to be in the right. The Bible text doesn't indicate whether Queen Vashti conveyed a reason for her refusal. It simply says she didn't come. A little communication could have gone a long way. A lack of communication usually leads to offense because the other person's imagination and emotions are allowed to paint their own inflammatory story.

Though a woman has the capacity to stand on her own and throw her own party in life, she needs to remain sensitive to the needs of her partner. She needs to be aware of when to switch her focus back to him. Distraction is a powerful weapon in the hands of the enemy, and through it he has destroyed many relationships. In the heat of the moment when we are busy, that's when the needs of our loved ones are easy to overlook or ignore—and the results can be devastating.

The question remains that if Queen Vashti knew the law about not appearing in public, knew that her husband was inebriated, and thought she was doing the right thing by saving them both from disgrace, why wouldn't she have sent him a note to that effect? She could have reminded him of the situation and given him an opportunity to reconsider. Then he would have been empowered to make the choice either to do the right thing or break his own law with a full understanding of what he was doing. Ah, but Queen Vashti didn't do that. We don't know how she worded her refusal. We simply know that girlfriend didn't show up at her man's party.

I'm sure that in the heat of the moment our beautiful queen didn't think about the impact of her decision. Few of us usually do at times like that. When our attention is divided or we might be offended, we tend to put out the immediate fire without realizing the mark it might leave behind. All Queen Vashti knew was she wasn't going to do what he asked. Perhaps she was influenced by the other women at her party. They may have encouraged her not to go as comeuppance for being ignored for so long. Perhaps she figured she would discuss it with him later.

Little did she realize the bigger issues her behavior raised. Little did she know the very core of her man's manhood had been challenged—and publicly. In light of his public disgrace and his anger, there was little chance he would handle it well. He had to defend his honor immediately. He had to reassert himself as a man and as the king. His boys—the nobles—seconded him. They wanted to protect their manhood too. So after getting advice from the peanut gallery, King Ahasuerus couldn't really turn back even if he wanted to. That would have made him lose even more face. No, Queen Vashti had to be made an example of. He couldn't—he wouldn't—let her affront slide. Everyone was watching, and what he did would affect the kingdom at large.

Ladies, we have to be careful not to put our men in positions that push them to defend themselves against us in public. Our homes are mini kingdoms. We must keep in mind that our actions at home also affect our men's kingdoms at large. What we do within our personal households slowly penetrates into our man's sphere of influence—and ours too. Eventually it may resonate in everything we do, throwing our relationships and our lives off balance. On a larger scale, what happens in our homes can seep into our communities and eventually might resonate throughout a nation, affecting the state of affairs in the world. We are all connected. Everything everywhere ultimately affects everyone. Like the vibrations of a butterfly's wings halfway across the world that sets pressure waves in motion that eventually add up to even more motion, which affects the weather and can lead to tidal waves, so do our choices and interactions release things into the atmosphere that affect others more than we know.

We could speculate from now to eternity. We really don't know why Vashti didn't comply with her husband's request. We're only told she did not. Who's to say if egos and attitudes were not involved? We only know her decision cost her greatly.

The overriding principle here is that submission is a beautiful thing. "Wives, submit to your own husbands" are powerful words for a powerful principle (Ephesians 5:22). In no way is godly submission an order to be a doormat. Instead, it's an invitation to voluntarily place yourself in a position to receive blessings. When we submit to God's order and agree with God, we are blessed. As we partner and become team players with our spouses, we are blessed. There is power in walking in agreement.

The Bible says that when God looked down on the people, He said, "Behold, they are one people...and nothing that they propose to do will now be impossible for them" (Genesis 11:6). This is the essence of submission. When we walk together in agreement, submitting to one another in love, we move forward and build kingdoms that endure. And submission is not one-sided. Men and women are both called to submission. "Be filled with the Spirit...submitting to one another out of reverence for Christ" (Ephesians 5:18,21).

In a healthy relationship, the choices we make are seldom about just us or our mates. We are modeling God's principles and revealing His blessings. These positives affect the people around us and encourage them to change and grow also. Our relationships reflect a larger picture called the kingdom of God, and they serve as an invitation for others to enter into a relationship with Him because we show them what the kingdom looks like.

Reflections

✻ In what ways do you struggle with "submission"?

✻ In what ways will submitting to your mate positively affect your relationship?

✻ How can the harmony in your relationship influence people around you?

Love Talk

Submission is not a weak or passive act. It is an active decision to choose agreement over strife, to choose blessings over hardship, to choose to be a team player over individual rights. In a relationship, mutual submission enables both of you to look out for the other and grow.

Part 2

Who Are You?

*Y*ou are a queen, a woman created to walk with a king. The Word of God tells us that woman was created for man, not the man for the woman (1 Corinthians 11:9). This is not an insult! In fact, it is high praise. Man needed woman. "But remember that in God's plan men and women need each other. For although the first woman came out of man, all men have been born from women ever since, and both men and women come from God their Creator" (verses 11-12 TLB).

That's right. Every person on the face of the earth now must pass through the womb of a woman. The man may start the process, but it is the woman who completes man's mandate to fill the earth by being the one who carries and births the harvest of what he planted. The next time you feel insignificant, take a look around you. See all those people? Remind yourself that the world as you know it would not exist without the presence of women. Ultimately, both the man and the woman can do nothing apart from God, but in quite a literal sense, we are God's gifts to each other.

Man cannot complete his God-given assignments without woman. Perhaps this is why the Word says, "He who finds a wife finds a good thing and obtains favor from the LORD" (Proverbs 18:22). It is a good thing because he will now be able to walk in the fullness of his God-given assignments. He will obtain favor for fulfilling these mandates. Favor comes either from pleasing God or at His sole discretion in accordance with His plan and will.

If you have an assignment that seems greater than your ability, don't despair. In His goodness, God never gives you an assignment without the means to fulfill it. Woman was part of the "missing equipment" man needed to walk in total obedience with God's design. It was God who said it wasn't good for the man to be alone. It was God who provided a helper for man (Genesis 2:18). A helper to help the man carry out his mandates. A helper qualified for this position to help fill the empty gaps in man's soul. A helper to be strong where he was weak. A helper who could be an able assistant in times when the man couldn't stand alone. And this works both ways, of course. This is why Scripture says, "Two are better than one, because they have a good reward for their labor" (Ecclesiastes 4:9 NKJV).

In a world where so many downplay the significance of women, it's important to recognize that God sees women as powerful additions to the world. Adam called his wife Eve "because she was the mother of all living" (Genesis 3:20).

It was this same Eve who got her husband to eat the fruit he knew he'd been instructed by God not to ingest. Adam knew it, and yet he chose to listen to his wife over obeying God. Though we know this wasn't a good thing, it does reveal a very significant fact. Not only did God create woman in such a manner that she would take a man's breath away, but He also armed her with a very powerful gift: influence.

While many women complain about the technicalities of submission, the power of influence has been sorely overlooked. While many chafe at why man was rated king, why man is the one in authority over woman, at the end of the day *influence* is more powerful than authority. Influence affects the mindset, the attitude, the will of a person. Influence can alter the choices a person makes despite that person wielding authority over the influencer.

Though God has ultimate authority, people break His command-ments every day. Why? Because of the power of influence. "The heart is the most deceitful thing there is and desperately wicked. No one can really know how bad it is!" (Jeremiah 17:9 TLB). Even the mighty apostle Paul said, "No matter which way I turn I can't make myself do right. I want to but I can't. When I want to do good, I don't; and when I try not to do wrong, I do it anyway" (Romans 7:18-19 TLB). Let's face it. We know what is right and what is wrong. It's just a matter of what we choose to do.

So where does influence place you in the mix of your man's king-dom and what it takes for him to rule well and be your king by your desire and not default? Where you are placed on a pedestal where you belong? Where you are treated as the true queen you were created to be? You see, a real queen is aware of her position. She understands it is her birthright. If she was not born into the position, then she knows she was chosen, which is even more powerful. She was desired and cho-sen on purpose to take her position.

As a queen, she is aware of the power of her office and her authority. She understands the atmosphere must change when she enters a room because of her extraordinary presence. She knows the power of her words. She knows that when she speaks, her words make things hap-pen. She uses her position with prudence and discretion. She doesn't make her husband sorry he made her queen.

A queen knows how to treat a king. After all, the world is watching. She leads by example. A true queen knows her life isn't her own. Instead, it is lived for the benefit of the entire kingdom. With this resolve firmly intact in her heart, how she conducts herself with her king and how she raises their children are done in light of how her household affects the kingdom at large. Her deeds will be heralded in the gates, her good works will testify of her spirit, and her family will rise up and call her blessed (Proverbs 31).

In no way does this woman feel powerless. She knows the effects she has on the people around her. She walks circumspectly, carefully thinking before she speaks and acts because she knows the lasting effects of her words and that her actions carry much weight. Looking down through history, we find Deborah, a judge of Israel, encouraging General Barak to fight to save the nation (Judges 4:4-8). We see Esther prevailing on her king to save the Jewish people (Esther 7:3-6). We see a wise woman on a city wall who avoided war against her city by wisely counseling the leaders of her community to hand over the enemy hiding within (2 Samuel 20:14-22). Women saving communities and nations!

The wife of Pontius Pilate relayed a dream she had to encourage her husband from being involved in the crucifixion of the Messiah. Women at work, securing the security and well-being of their men, children, and communities. This is who we are.

Though man and woman were given the same mandates from God, the burden falls primarily on the man to complete them. God holds the man responsible for not only fulfilling his assignment but for securing the woman's alignment with God's instructions. Adam was held responsible for Eve's disobedience in the garden though she was subject to her own personal consequences for her sin. As wives we empower our husbands to be whom God created them to be. We assist them in fulfilling their God-given mandates that date back to the Garden of Eden. As mothers, we help our children know their gifts, we nurture their dreams, and we direct them toward their God-given destinies. As sisters in the Lord we correct, encourage, and celebrate one another. As friends we walk and speak the truth in love, displaying the law of kindness while granting support.

And as we fulfill the fullness of our calling as women, our dreams are birthed and come true. Living and being who we were created by God to be opens endless doors of opportunity to make a difference, help people know God, and prosper. God's joy and peace come with the understanding of who we are and how we are to live within the parameters of His design. This eliminates the struggle so many people in the world have to establish their identities. Ours has already been set up according to God's design. And it is perfect. As we confess our sins and accept Jesus's wonderful gift of salvation, we are redeemed from the curse of sin and our own waywardness.

A true queen knows her God. Because of this, she is strong and accomplishes much more than she's ever dreamed. She willingly leaves room in her world for her man to be her king. She empowers the people around her to rise and live out their fullest, God-given potential. She's a credit to her family and the world at large. And that is what being a queen and influencing a kingdom is all about.

5

Will the Real Queen Arise?

*"We suggest that, subject to your agreement, you issue a royal
edict, a law of the Medes and Persians that can never be
changed, that Queen Vashti be forever banished from your
presence and that you choose another queen more worthy than
she"... The king and his nobles thought this made good sense, so
he followed Memucan's counsel. He sent letters to all parts of
the empire, to each province in its own script and language,
proclaiming that every man should be the ruler of his own home
and should say whatever he pleases (Esther 1:19,21-22 NLT).*

I'm sure it seemed like a good idea at the time. After all, Vashti
had disgraced the king in public. But now that he missed her so
deeply, King Ahasuerus was left to ponder the errors that resulted from
his angry outburst. He knew he loved Vashti, and now he missed her.
Because of his edict, he'd boxed himself into a corner. Besides, Memucan had raised a good point when he essentially said, "Do we want a
country of women who don't know their place?" Along with banish-
ing Vashti, the king had sent out a proclamation that said, "Every husband should be the master of his home and speak with final authority"
(Esther 1:22 GNT). And kings could not go back on their word. Everything the king had written or that was written under his authority was
established and couldn't be reversed.

The king knew he was brooding, but he couldn't help it. He wanted his queen back. Memucan had said he deserved a queen who was better than Queen Vashti, someone more worthy than she. Was there such a woman? And what would such a woman look like?

He looked up to survey the serious faces before him. His closest counsel. These were his friends as well as his advisors. He trusted them. They stood before him in a united front. He asked them how he should go about finding a new queen.

They studied their king's face as they weighed their words before delivering them:

> Let beautiful young virgins be sought out for the king. And let the king appoint officers in all the provinces of his kingdom to gather all the beautiful young virgins to the harem in Susa the capital, under custody of Hegai, the king's eunuch, who is in charge of the women. Let their cosmetics be given them. And let the young woman who pleases the king be queen instead of Vashti (Esther 2:2-4).

The king could feel himself feeling lighter and his mood lifting already in anticipation. Yes, it was a good idea! This time he would be clear about what he was looking for. He had access to the most choice women in the kingdom. The variety was endless! And these women would love to be considered by him. After all, who wouldn't want to be the wife of a king? Especially one as powerful as he? This time he would be more careful. Out of all the women he could have had, he'd been seduced by the beauty of Vashti. At the time he'd not thought to research her character, think of what type of wife she would be, or what impact her character might have on his reputation and his kingdom. No, he had thought of none of those issues. He'd been captivated by her external assets. He shook his head at the thought. Obviously beauty was not enough.

❧❧❧

The book of Proverbs is quick to note that "charm is deceptive, and beauty is fleeting; but a woman who fears the Lord is to be praised"

(Proverbs 31:30 NIV). In a world obsessed with beauty, it is easy to become distracted from what matters most—character. At the end of the day, even the most beautiful woman can be seen as unattractive if she doesn't conduct herself according to God's design for her life. There are countless scriptures pointing to how foolishness and lack of prudence and discretion can mar the otherwise flawless finish of a woman's beauty. Add to that the various cautions regarding a nagging wife and words spoken in haste, and we have a vivid picture of traits none of us want to be associated with. "Like a gold ring in a pig's snout is a beautiful woman without discretion" (Proverbs 11:22). "It is better to live alone in the desert than with a quarrelsome, complaining wife" (Proverbs 21:19 NLT). I'm sure none of us want to be associated with adorning pigs or chasing men into the desert.

The truth of the matter is, a woman cannot be a queen if her man doesn't look like a king. And she has a lot to do with how her man looks and behaves. The "woman is the glory of man," Scripture tells us in 1 Corinthians 11:7 (NIV). "Glory" here speaks of the evidence of the man's presence and power at work in her life. When we see a good-looking woman dressed beautifully and with a glowing countenance, we think not only does she take care of herself but also that her husband has done well by her. If she looked bad, we would wonder why her husband wasn't providing better for her. As man was meant to represent God in the earth, the woman was meant to represent her husband.

What you do affects your man's image and vice versa. This is why it is noted that the Proverbs 31 woman's husband was spoken of well at the gates (verse 23). There is no mistake or oversight on this being a pointed part of the text after listing all of the woman's attributes. The inference is that because of who she was, her husband was who he was. She had a direct impact on his well-being, which contributed to him being an upstanding citizen. She sent him out into the world well armed in the confirmation of who he was as a man. He knew he had a support system that kept him sound in mind and body so he could handle his business without distraction and operate in full integrity.

As men are considered today for political office or a major job promotion, such as a partner at a law firm, dinners are often hosted and events attended to give the business partners opportunities to peruse the partner of the prospective partner. In big business, it's understood that a man's judgment will be as sound as the stability of his home and the clarity of his thoughts. If it looks as if the wife is a loose cannon, that might affect his opportunities negatively. He may be deemed an undesirable candidate because the partners consider the stability of their personnel vital to the stability of their business.

Lady, are you still not convinced of your power of influence? Wars have been fought over women. Crimes have been committed over women. Men have sacrificed or lost all they have over women. Cities have also been conquered or saved because of women. Acts of bravery have been performed for women.

The myth is that a woman must choose either beauty or smarts. But may I go on record saying that most men find humble smarts truly beautiful in women? Yes, husbands want beauty on the outside, but they would also like to know they can confide in their wives about the things they struggle with and get sound counsel and positive feedback. After all, if their wives, their confidantes, the people who know them best can't speak into their lives, then what do they have in the end? Yes, a trophy wife will get old quickly. Beauty alone will never sustain a relationship, especially since eventually we all age and physical beauty gradually declines. An emphasis on outer beauty alone places a wife in danger of being replaced by a younger model.

Another important area to understand is that men need different things in the different stages of their lives. As a man matures, he needs his woman to mature so their relationship, level of communication, partnership, and love deepen. The normal husband longs for security within his personal space. He likes to know that everything is under control in his home because the emergencies of life are sufficient to deal with. He needs an oasis where he can relax, let down his guard, be himself, and be free from competition. The last person he wants to contend with is his wife. He needs an "I've got your back" kind of wife. Whether he is right or wrong, his wife—his queen—needs to know how to handle every situation with her husband with discretion and finesse. A true queen knows her power and wields the scepter carefully and positively.

Reflections

❧ What is your attitude, posture, and behavior when your man isn't necessarily right in a situation?

❧ How would you evaluate your ability to communicate with your partner?

❧ In what ways do you help your man feel safe with you?

Love Talk

> Who can find a virtuous and capable wife?
> She is more precious than rubies.
> Her husband can trust her,
>   and she will greatly enrich his life.
> She brings him good, not harm,
>   all the days of her life
>
> (Proverbs 31:10-12 NLT).

6

Set Apart for Destiny

As a result of the king's decree, Esther, along with many other young women, was brought to the king's harem at the fortress of Susa and placed in Hegai's care...Hegai was very impressed with Esther and treated her kindly. He quickly ordered a special menu for her and provided her with beauty treatments. He also assigned her seven maids specially chosen from the king's palace, and he moved her and her maids into the best place in the harem (Esther 2:8-9 NLT).

The women came from near and far. Young virgins untouched by men. The king would not accept leftovers or anything that had been enjoyed by another. He wanted a queen who was reserved for him and him alone. Tall, short, dark, and fair, the women were brought in. The court was alive and buzzing with activity as they entered the king's harem at the fortress of Susa.

The nobles were heard discussing how fortunate the king was to have such a bevy of beauties to choose from. Each had their own opinions as to whom the king would choose. Others speculated who would be chosen if it were their choice.

Among the women, one in particular seemed to stand out. There was something different about her. She didn't enter into the giddy conversations of the other young women. There was something...regal about her. Dark and mysterious, she was like a diamond that hadn't yet been polished, but the underlying brilliance could be anticipated.

The people saw the glint in Hegai's eyes as he perused this young woman. Though he was a eunuch, he had a most discriminating eye for beautiful women. Ah yes, there was something special about this one. Even better, it was apparent she didn't know her own beauty or the effect she was having on those who gazed upon her. She was neither self-conscious nor proud, neither plain nor flamboyant. There was an elegant humility about her mingled with quiet confidence. She put forth no posturing to impress. She had been chosen to be here. She was present because she had been commanded to appear. She gave the impression she would have been just as much at peace if still in her own home and not surrounded by the opulence and attention of the king's court.

Gracious and serene, she was intently studying her surroundings, betraying her intelligence and substance. This was a woman who thought before she spoke. It was apparent she wasn't cut from the same cloth as the others. Though they came from as faraway as India to as near as Susa, there was a sameness about them all except for this one.

Hegai hadn't lost his eye or his touch, the noblemen said as they chuckled among themselves. They watched him gently lead this woman away from the others. As he separated seven of the choicest king's maids to accompany her to the best quarters that were set apart from the rest, it was clear who was his candidate for the next queen. This separation was wise on Hegai's part. They all agreed that bad company corrupts good manners. This outstanding young woman should be set apart and special attention paid to grooming her for her position. The king was very particular about how he liked things done. She would have to be taught and prepared to be a suitable queen. Everyone agreed she already had a good start on the process. They wondered if she had any idea what her future held. No one could have prepared her for this day or the days to come. How she weathered the process of preparation would reveal if she was the queen they hoped she would be. Not every woman was able to stand alone, and yet as queen there would be times when she would have to. She could not live for the approval of others. She would be expected to set the standard. This called for a life of living apart from all that was common and normal. Few women were born for this or could handle it. They would see if she was. Yes, indeed, it was just a matter of time.

☙

Destiny takes time. It unfolds even while we are unaware. And yet God says before we were, He knew us. He set us apart for His purposes. He chooses us individually in accordance with His kingdom plan. Could it be that our little-girl dreams are borne in the heart of God first? All those princess fancies of being swept away by a dashing prince or, better yet, a king seated upon a gallant horse? Today that scenario occurs only in the movies, but here we see the scenario played out in real life in the Bible of all places!

I wonder what Esther's aspirations were? Her existence up to this point had been a simple one. She was an orphan who lived with her cousin Mordecai. He was a godly man who reminded her daily of the importance of maintaining her relationship with the God of Israel even though they lived as captives in a foreign land. Mordecai was a man of unshakeable faith and quiet dignity. He refused to allow the system around him to force him to compromise or bow to other gods. This attitude he also instilled in his young charge.

Then out of nowhere, Esther finds herself taken to the palace of the king of Persia to participate in the first-ever beauty contest. The prize? To be chosen as queen. Who could dream this scenario up on any given afternoon? And yet our lives unfold with unanticipated twists and turns. How we rise to the occasions betrays if we understand the true import of destiny and purpose. Wherever God places us, it is purposeful on His part. Whether single or married, we are where we are as part of a much larger and more intricate design than we will ever be aware of. With this thought in mind, we need to seize each day with a greater sense of purpose than ever before.

In the case of King Ahasuerus, Vashti had been his queen, but she'd been removed. It was a matter of destiny. Persia had a natural king.

But even if the people didn't know it or acknowledge it, they also had a supernatural king who used the natural king for His purposes and greater design. It is true that the hearts of kings are in God's hands. This time in history was to be Esther's moment. She was a key player in the hands of God. She would be central to the plot of His next move on behalf of His people exiled to the east. With this in mind, we can understand why Esther was met with great favor by Hegai. It was part of God's perfect will unfolding. Did Esther know her destiny? The fact that she was set apart to take part in something huge? I would say absolutely not. But God's plan would unfold as it does in all of our lives.

How does this pertain to us today? Marriage is not just an emotional call. It's also a matter of destiny—God's destiny for us. Two people in today's world come together based on what they call chemistry. In many cases, not much thought is given to the possibility or even certainty that God drew them together. Beyond how the two people feel, there should be an understanding of their relationship using their intellectual and spiritual faculties as well.

Yes, as a couple we love each other, but what is God's purpose for our union? In what way can we, as a couple, fulfill our God-given destinies? How do we become a power couple that can impact our world for the kingdom of God? How can our home be used as an epicenter for divine influence in our community? With these types of thoughts uppermost in our minds as individuals as well as couples, we will see the world changed one home at a time.

Esther was called to the palace, along with a great many other young women. But it was she who caught the eye of the king's head eunuch. It was she whom Hegai separated from the masses and gave special attendants and accommodations. When we've been set apart for a divine work, we can't continue to live the way others live. We can't do what they do or even walk with the people they walk with. In Esther's case, Hegai furnished her with seven attendants. (In the Bible, seven is the number of perfection and maturation.)

When we've been set apart for God's glory, our maturing is required. God is interested in our character development more than our success.

As we submit to being refined, He paves the way for greatness to occur in our relationships, in our professions, in every area of our lives. Sometimes when He has separated us from the masses, it may seem that the other people are having more fun. But at what expense? When Esther was separated from the others by special accommodations, it may have felt a bit lonely. Yet she was being groomed for greatness. What am I saying? There is a price to pay for divine placement. But by the end of the situation when all is revealed, the price we pay will never surpass the glory and rewards of God's plan.

Esther was being prepared to be a married woman. This required separation. Far too many married women try to maintain their single existence. This is never successful. No one can serve two masters. She will love one and despise the other. The single life must be released to enter into a fruitful marriage. Habits must change. Sometimes friends must change. Thinking must be renewed in some areas to experience the full transformation God has in mind for a woman in marriage. In marriage, a man and a woman become one. They are no longer individuals but a solid unit God can use to do powerful things for His kingdom. Serving God and being available for use by Him should be one of the goals of every marriage. Yes, personal satisfaction can be a goal, but that satisfaction should come from knowing you have been set apart from the others and chosen to come together as part of a divine destiny for a purpose greater than yourself. This is a privilege that has great rewards.

Reflections

✣ What gifts does your mate possess? For what purposes has God set your mate apart?

✣ In what ways do you see God setting you apart for your relationship? How do you believe He would like to use both of you together?

✣ What do you need to do differently to truly become one with your spouse?

Love Talk

"For this reason a man will leave his father and mother and be united to his wife, and the two will become one flesh" (Ephesians 5:31 NIV). And vice versa. There must be a forsaking of all others on the part of both people to begin the journey of becoming one. Being set apart is not a lonely place. It opens the door for the best things, people, and circumstances to be placed in your lives. Just as God has set you apart for your mate, He has also set your mate apart for you toward a common end.

Always remember that your marriage is more than just romance. It is two people set apart for God's purposes to utilize the gifts He's placed in both of you. As you focus on the higher purpose for your union, encouraging each other to good works, you will become the power couple God wants you to be.

7

The Real Treatment

*Hegai was very impressed with Esther and treated her
kindly. He quickly ordered a special menu for her and
provided her with beauty treatments (Esther 2:9 NLT).*

Hegai made his way down the corridor with Esther following
behind him. His arms waving, he signaled attendants, and
they scurried to do his bidding. He glanced back to give her a reassuring smile, the light of approval shining in his eyes. She was so beautiful. Oh yes, she would be perfect. He would see to that. He'd selected for her seven choice maids from the king's court. They would teach her everything she needed to know about palace protocols and even about the king himself. Hegai wanted her well prepared for her first meeting with the monarch.

While some of the other young women had gazed around them with fear and apprehension, this young woman hadn't seemed intimidated by her surroundings. He wondered at her background. Nothing about her appearance or bearing betrayed her origin. At any rate, he didn't care. He was sold. She was his candidate for queen, and he would do everything in his power to make it happen. She would want for nothing. The first thing he must do is separate her from the rest of the young women lest any bad company among them corrupt her manners. He wanted to be her main influence. He would teach her everything she needed to know to get the king's attention and please him. Oh, many of the young ladies that had been brought to the palace would be capable of getting the king's attention. They were lovely enough. But to *keep* his attention—this would take more than beauty. It would take wisdom, wit, and the right combination of feminine charms. Hegai had sized Esther up and decided that while she seemed quite self-confident, she would also be a teachable student. She would be able to discern when and how to apply what he would teach her.

As he led her to the best apartments in the harem, he gave instructions about her diet and the beauty treatments she was to receive. Twelve months of being washed, soaked, and bathed in costly oils and perfumes. She was beautiful, yes, but she must measure up to all the standards of the king. With so many women gathered from so many different provinces across the king's vast empire, the variety of beauty, smells, traits, and attributes were wide ranging. This was expected as these things had everything to do with diet, environment, and upbringing. It would take an extraordinary woman to stand out. And since the king was used to a certain style, standard, and even smell, it was crucial that Esther appeal to all his senses.

Her diet must also be changed. After all we are what we eat. Everything about this woman had to be pleasing to the king—internally and externally. Hegai didn't want the king to find one fault with Esther. He opened the door to her living quarters with a great sweep of his arms as if to say, "Voila!"

Esther's eyes took in the room, perusing every corner.

Hegai watched her. This one was truly different. She didn't ask inane questions or make conversation just for the sake of chasing away nervousness. She hadn't tried to curry favor. She was downright regal this one. He studied her as she studiously made her way past the foyer to the main greeting hall.

Walking slowly forward, Esther reached the center of the room and turned toward him clasping her hands before her. She took a deep breath, exhaling slowly, her head rising as if asserting herself in her new surroundings, giving her own vote of approval that yes, these accommodations were acceptable.

Hegai wondered if she'd ever seen such finery before. At that moment she looked as if she were quite accustomed to it. He knew without a doubt that she was the one. Yes, indeed. She looked and acted like a queen.

✺

Who knows the day or the hour when we will walk into our destiny? It's only when we look back in hindsight do we discover when we stepped on that "X marks the spot" in the spirit. Do you remember the moment you met your man and the moment you knew he was "the one"? And now the more you walk together, the more you realize that perhaps you'd been groomed your entire lifetime to be with this person. I believe long before we meet our intended partners, God has begun the work of refining and preparing us to be "helpmeets" for them. God alone knows the needs of the men He is preparing us for, and He works to prepare us and them. Just as he fashioned Eve while Adam slept, He has also fashioned you to be the perfect complement to your God-given assignment of a mate. Yes, that man is an assignment. God has entrusted that man to your care. He designed you to be your man's "good thing" (Proverbs 18:22). Your presence in his life is going to help him garner favor as your love and influence strengthen him to be everything he was created to be.

Ah, but first you must be prepared. Let's take a look at where you're living spiritually. Your relationship will exist within the capacity of your faith. Why is this important to understand? Because you're going to have to trust the Lord to keep your man and your relationship strong. Today there is an all-out assault against marriage and the sanctity of it. These are perilous times for relationships. Faithfulness is at an all-time low.

When it comes to your relationship, you can either live in expectancy of your mate disappointing you and being unfaithful or you can walk in the assurance that God has blessed you with a man who recognizes your value and holds his covenant with you in sacred trust. Of course, we are speaking here of a man who is accountable to God. When your man doesn't want to break God's heart, he won't want to break yours either. If he loves the Lord with all his heart, soul, mind, and strength, he will honor his covenant with you and not compromise your relationship. Choose to live within the realm of God's ability to protect your marriage and keep it secure as you both honor Christ. Perhaps your mate isn't surrendered to Christ. God will sanctify him, set him apart, and keep him for you as you walk in prayerful faith, trusting God to not only keep your man but transform him into a man of faith.

Second, let's look at the company you keep. The great mistake most married women make is to keep company with women who are either unhappy in their marriages or not married. This may lead you to the Desperate Housewives Club or the Being Envious of Single Women's Freedom Club. You can't give your marriage the attention it needs if you're unhappy or if you're still living as a single. It won't work. You want to make sure your friends honor marriage—especially your marriage commitment—enough to encourage you to do those things that will nourish your marriage.

Third, let's consider your diet. What are you eating? Jesus said it is not what goes in but what comes out of the mouth that defiles us (Matthew 15:11). I believe we get to choose our physical, spiritual, and emotional diet, and that what we take in has a lot to do with what comes out of us. If we have ingested a lot of negative experiences, it will affect our thinking, which will affect our attitudes, our conversations, and our actions. There is a work of purification that needs to take place in the diet of every person who longs to be joined to another. We can't afford to make bitterness, unforgiveness, rejection, and fear part of our diet. Those will sour our relationships. Instead, let's eat the fruit of the Spirit, and allow it to become an unconscious part of who we are. "The fruit of the Spirit is love, joy, peace, patience, kindness, goodness, faithfulness, gentleness, self-control" (Galatians 5:22-23). Let it flavor our character so that not only are our romantic relationships sweet, but all our relationships reflect the Holy Spirit.

Last but certainly not least, let's consider our personal toilette. Did you notice it took 12 months of baths with oils and perfumes to prepare these candidates for the king? In biblical terms, 12 is considered the number of establishment. In their case, reestablishment. They had lived one type of life, but now they were brought into Susa to live with the king. Their world as they knew it no longer existed. They had literally come out of the world and into his personal sphere. They were in the world but no longer *of* the common world.

We also make that transition when we come to Christ. This change requires a new way of thinking, speaking, and living. The old rules no longer apply, and a new way of approaching life must be embraced. These women were washed and saturated in the ways of the king's personal domain. The fragrances were heady. Like the beauty treatments the women went through, we go through a cleansing and beautification through the fruit of the Spirit.

God wants to wash us and perfume us with His Spirit. There is nothing more attractive than a man or a woman who is full of "love, joy, peace, patience, kindness, goodness, faithfulness, gentleness, self-control." These can only come from digesting the Word of God and allowing it to become part of us. His Word is meat for our souls. He is the bread of life; His Spirit is the wellspring of living water that continually refreshes and renews us to face every twist and turn in our relationships and in our lives.

Relationships are one of the few jobs in life we don't study for. Marriage comes with no manual, and yet it is critical for us to master this vital part of our lives. God wants to prepare us just as He fashioned Eve that lovely afternoon in the Garden of Eden. When He'd completed His work, He presented her to Adam. Adam was quick to recognize, claim, and name his new companion. There was never a doubt in his mind that she was the one he'd been looking for when he was naming all the animals. It was resoundingly clear that she was bone of his bone, flesh of his flesh, specially crafted and prepared just for him. The man in your life should feel the same way about you.

Reflections

✼ In what ways did God prepare you for your mate?

✼ Are any of your friendships or associations negatively impacting you or your marriage? How can you change that?

❧ How is your spiritual diet? What do you need more of to nourish your relationship with God and with your mate?

Love Talk

"Love is patient, love is kind. It does not envy, it does not boast, it..." well, you know the rest from 1 Corinthians 13:4-8. But how can we develop and master all those wonderful attributes? We know they won't just show up in our lives overnight. So how do we instill them inside us? By carefully steeping ourselves in the Word of God and renewing our minds so that God can transform us into the women He created us to be. This comes when we surrender our will to His and, with His help, apply the discipline it takes to master self-control so we will become the fruitful and loving wives that nourish the hearts of our men and bring out the King within them.

8

How to Be Chosen

When the young woman went in to the king…she was given whatever she desired to take with her from the harem to the king's palace…When the turn came for Esther…to go in to the king, she asked for nothing except what Hegai the king's eunuch, who had charge of the women, advised. Now Esther was winning favor in the eyes of all who saw her. And when Esther was taken to King Ahasuerus into his royal palace in the tenth month, which is the month of Tebeth, in the seventh year of his reign, the king loved Esther more than all the women, and she won grace and favor in his sight more than all the virgins, so that he set the royal crown on her head and made her queen instead of Vashti (Esther 2:13,15-17).

Esther watched the women come and the women go. It seemed the king's chambers were like a revolving door. One by one they went, hopeful that they would be the one chosen to be queen. After months of preparation, six months of treatments with oil of myrrh, spices, and perfumes the day came when they faced the reason they were all in the palace—not for their pleasure but for the pleasure of the king. If he was pleased with them, they would remain in his presence. If not, they would live in the concubine section of the harem. Some hoped for that, happy to settle for the benefits of living in the kingdom without responsibility, while others were distraught when it was obvious they weren't the king's choice.

Esther wasn't sure what to expect or what she wanted the outcome to be. She left her future completely in God's hands. That was what Mordecai had always taught her to do. For now she was happy for the privacy of her own apartments. There, in-between the beauty treatments, she could take time to pray and meditate with God on her future. She would not allow the heady surroundings to make her forget where she came from and what was most important. Though there was a possibility that she could be the next queen, she knew that she was first a child of God. She was aware that everything around her was in opposition to her faith and what she knew about God's ways. For instance, her Jewish name was Hadassah, but now she was called Esther, after a Babylonian goddess called Ishtar. Ishtar was the queen of love. The Babylonians and Persians paid homage to her, along with many other gods.

Esther had heard about King Ahasuerus. He was a heathen in the eyes of the Jews. He didn't worship the one true God like they did. And yet she was one of the king's subjects. She was required to give him honor. Her fate lay in his hands. At his command she would be queen or live as a concubine. At his command she could live or die. Though she didn't fear him, she knew she must respect him. She decided all she could do was be the best woman she knew to be. This would honor God and, hopefully, be conciliatory to the king.

Finally the knock came, signaling it was her turn to spend the night with the king. It felt like Hegai had been preparing her for this moment forever. This was it. She'd been told she could take whatever she wanted with her to the king's chambers, but she was at a loss as to what that would be. She searched Hegai's eyes and then asked for his direction. What should she take? What could she possibly offer the king that he didn't already have…besides herself? That was the only gift she knew to give. And so she stood still and allowed Hegai to fuss over her one last time—adjusting the folds of her gown and wiping away an imaginary strand of hair from her cheek.

She was perfect, he said. And then he offered her some last-minute advice on what to take and what to do.

She felt far from ready and very nervous as she walked toward the king's chambers. She could feel the stares following her down the corridor. Taking a deep breath, she paused as the king's servants opened the king's chamber doors before her. Her eyes adjusted to the light after she entered, and the king came into view. Bowing deeply she raised her eyes to look into his eyes. And then she smiled. The king was, after all, just a man.

~~eeQ₯₯e~~

Do you know the end of the story? Esther found favor in the eyes of the king and was crowned queen. She was the winner of the first beauty contest. As in modern pageants, after the parade of contestants in swimsuits and evening gowns has been followed by the talent contest, it comes down to the character and intelligence of the candidates. As they are asked to express their views on a given subject, the judges rate them, and then they tally their votes. Even in mainstream beauty pageants, character and intelligence are important factors for any queen to possess. After all, she will be representing the state, the country, or perhaps the universe, depending on the level of the contest!

Bringing this home, after all the beauty rituals are over and you've captured the eyes of a man, the acid test will be whether you also capture his heart. Can you keep his interest and respect? It's been said that a man falls in love with a woman based on how he feels when he is with her. Could it be that Esther went about capturing the king's attention in a way the previous candidates did not? Could it be that she took the time to find out more about the king?

If she was to be his queen, she would need to know him well—and not through hearsay. She would need to find out what he liked and what he didn't like. What did he dream about at night? What made him joyful? What was he passionate about? A woman who knows how to draw a man out will more easily capture his heart.

Every question asked about him or his preferences gives him a greater feeling of significance. This woman cares about who he is. Within his personal space, though he is the king of his world, he longs to be his woman's king most of all. To feel that his presence in his woman's life is hugely important.

I have the feeling that perhaps the other young women, armed with whatever props they chose, went in and focused on telling the king all about themselves. You know, giving a real sales pitch. Have you ever listened to someone go on and on about him- or herself? Pretty boring, isn't it? Have you noticed how alive you feel when someone asks you questions about the things that are important to you? It feels good to be cared about and listened to. It feels like you hold significance for the other person. It builds the thought that you can interact with this person and contribute something to his or her life. Men need this. They must have it. The need has been built into their spirits to care for people they love and to cover and protect them.

A man needs to know he's needed, but he also needs to feel honored. Part of his validation as a man comes from his woman. As she honors him, he rises to the occasion and chooses to take care of her, to protect her, to cherish her as the precious gift she is.

We don't know what actually transpired between Esther and the king that night. But the Bible tells us that Esther took only what Hegai advised her to take. No specifics are given. Perhaps it was a small token or gift for the king. Esther needed no extra adornment; her beauty was well established. Even the women approved of her looks as she made her way to the king that night. We are simply told that the king was pleased with her. He chose Esther for his queen. Did you get that? Esther didn't choose the king. She was presented to him. She was made available to him. She accepted his attentions, and he chose her.

It is so critical for a man to choose his queen. That way he will always know that this was the woman of his choosing. If he ever feels manipulated or pulled into a relationship he didn't initiate, there will be a question in his mind of whether he made the choice…or the best choice. He will wonder if there was someone else out there for him if he didn't have to pursue, fight for, and win his woman, his elusive prize.

This pursuit also builds confidence in the heart of a woman. To know that this man really wants her, comes after her, and focuses on winning her heart helps her relax in his love. She doesn't have to strive for his attention. There is nothing to prove. She is a wanted woman!

Esther was wanted and chosen. I credit her incredible restraint above her beauty for this. There was no desperation in her body language or countenance. She was willing to take or leave the king. She wasn't anxious because she had nothing to prove. She was simply who she was. Take it or leave it. This freed her to focus on the king and let him know she wanted to know more about him, to make him feel like the king he was.

And the king was released to love and celebrate Esther because he felt celebrated.

The morning brought great fanfare as Esther was chosen to be queen. A great celebration was thrown, including gifts for all in attendance, in honor of Esther.

At the end of the day, our love relationships should be celebrations of each other. This only happens when we realize the relationships are not about us. Instead, it is about the people we love. As we celebrate our partners by giving them the significance they so deeply need, we are celebrated in return. Love is continually renewed as we make this a daily exchange. This is one of the secrets to truly being a queen.

Reflections

❧ In what ways do you practice restraint with your partner?

❧ Whose needs do you focus on most in your relationship?

❧ In what ways do you make your partner feel significant?

Love Talk

It is not how you feel that will make the true difference in your relationship. It is how you make your mate feel. You will only experience as much joy as your spouse experiences. In this way, you can set the tone in your home for love and open exchanges that will nurture romance and passion.

Part 3

Who Is Your Enemy?

The reality of life is we are in a war. And it is up to us to choose which side of the battle we're on. For those who have chosen to be daughters of Zion, who call God their "Abba Father" through association with Jesus, the reality of the enemy is forefront in every area of our lives. That we have an enemy we must never deny. Armed with this knowledge, we can live offensively. We don't always have to be in a state of emergency, putting out fires in our lives after the enemy attacks. When we know we have an enemy, we take on a different posture as we approach life. We won't be shaken or shocked when an attack comes. We expect it and are ready to fight back, to engage in the necessary warfare alongside God and claim victory in Him.

When Gideon was preparing for war, God instructed him to weed out the men who weren't ready for war by the posture they took when drinking water from a brook. He told Gideon to select those who drank the water from cupped hands rather than stooping down to the brook (Judges 7:5). Why did God do that? Because He needed men who would never relax, who would always be alert and aware of what was going on around them.

God wants us to have the same posture. He wants us to be alert because our enemy is a roaring lion seeking people to devour (1 Peter 5:8). He wants to devour our heart for worship, our obedience to God, the fruit of our hands, and our healthy relationships that honor God. The enemy is Satan. The war he wages isn't directed against us personally. We are merely pawns in his vendetta against God. He knows the best way to hurt God is to get us to hurt ourselves and other Christians by not obeying God's instructions. Through our disobedience and lack of surrender to God, we open the door for Satan to rob us of the very blessings God wants to give us. God is grieved when this happens.

When I was in high school, there was a girl who didn't like me. She was a friend of the daughter of my little brother's babysitter. One day when she went there, she found out that Ian was my little brother. She hit him and made him cry! Because she hated me, she struck out against who she knew I loved. It was an attempt to upset and hurt me. And she accomplished her goal. I was upset, but I was also shocked at the depth of venom she had in her heart against me. It was a hatred so deep she would strike a helpless child who had nothing to do with the issue between us. This is the heart of Satan. The same hatred that causes him to strike out against us as he seeks vengeance against God fuels his agenda. He wants to cause us great hurt. At the heart of the greatest pain for God and us is the destruction of loving relationships. Satan believes destroying our loving relationships will cripple our ability to be fruitful and multiply as ordained by God.

The devil's acts against us started in the Garden of Eden, with Eve, and continue to the present. After persuading Eve to partake of the fruit she'd been warned to not eat and then getting her to influence her husband to eat also, the battle lines were clearly drawn. God proclaimed that the serpent would be cursed and nip at the heel of woman's offspring, while her offspring would bruise his head. And man would find working the field difficult now, which was a new experience for him.

The bottom line? The attempt of the man and woman to be independent from God caused them—and us—great difficulty from that day forward. What had been originally ordained to be easy for them was now to be borne through great effort. The fruit of Eve's womb, the work of their hands, and their relationship would suffer great stress. This would help keep them dependent on God as never before. The irony that their attempt at independence rendered them even more dependent on God shouldn't be lost. We need God in our lives to help us successfully navigate the day-to-day interactions that make us fruitful, whether it be in the boardroom or the bedroom. We can't do it alone! In our weaknesses, God is made strong, taking up our part and championing us across the finish line to healthy relationships, joyful interactions, and peace in every area of our lives (2 Corinthians 12:9; 2 Timothy 4:7). Because we are right with Him, we are made right with others. Because of His love for us, we are enabled to love more fully and unconditionally. We utilize His love to love others—even the people we might consider unlovable.

I had a friend who once told me that when she was in a good place in her relationship with God, her relationship with her spouse was exceptional. She was able to love him no matter what was going on between them. But if her relationship with God was dry and not in a good place, her relationship with her beloved suffered. The enemy knows we are designed to be conduits of God's love toward one another. That is why he is so focused on interrupting our interactions. No matter where we find ourselves in life, we must not be ignorant of Satan's devices.

Now that we know his motives, we must also be aware that Satan will stop at nothing to achieve his ends. That's all the more reason for us to be committed to our loving relationships with new intensity. Knowing that the demise of our relationship with God, our mates, and those God has placed in our lives is food for someone else's vengeance should help us be even more passionate about practicing the fruit of the Spirit and the power of restraint, forgiveness, and reconciliation no matter what the cost. Maintaining and preserving our relationships is the best testimony against God's enemy we can achieve.

This is the atmosphere Esther found herself in. Having become queen, she now faced a hateful man who was determined to destroy the Jews, not because of anything they had done to him but merely to get back at one man who refused to honor him (Esther 3:5-6). In Haman's mind, *all* the Jews should pay for the wrongs of one man named Mordecai.

God's mind works exactly opposite of His enemy's. God asked Jesus to become a man and take on the sins (wrongs) of all people for the sake of saving us all. We are all Esthers caught up in a similar drama. We become the central characters in our own play with the audience of heaven watching with great anticipation how our relationships will play out. The important thing we need to know is that the end of our story is reached with the help of God. We do not give in to despair, fear, pride, unforgiveness, or hopelessness. With God's help, we recognize the twists and turns in the plot, and we make the correct adjustments to bring reconciliation and restoration. In the end, we are fruitful and God is glorified because we displayed what true kingdom living looks like. Our lives and relationships encourage people to thirst for a relationship with God as they see in us the joys and benefits of serving Him. This is how we multiply our faith. We add to the kingdom of heaven through the success of our relationships here on earth. This is true fruitfulness.

We want to achieve the highest degree of kingdom living here on earth. We want to live in an atmosphere of continual worship of our Lord Jesus Christ. This is what our King enjoys, and this is what blesses every queen. As these two states coexist according to God's design, the attempts of the enemy will be ineffective and peace will be maintained. All is well within our personal worlds.

9

The Power of Identity

Esther had not made known her kindred or her people, as
Mordecai had commanded her, for Esther obeyed Mordecai
just as when she was brought up by him (Esther 2:20)

Esther made her way down the main corridor of the king's apartments well aware of the admiring looks that lingered on her. She graciously nodded as she made her way back to her apartments. She still marveled at her new status. It was a fairy tale of epic proportions. She, a Jewish orphan, had been decreed queen of Persia. Never in her wildest dreams had she imagined she would find herself strolling through a palace with attendants at her beck and call.

Of course, she'd dreamed as most little girls did, that one day she would be married to a wonderful man who would love her passionately. But a king? Perhaps she'd even daydreamed about a knight in shining armor or a prince. But a king? A powerful king and reigning monarch of not one country, but several? Given the plight of her people, captured and in exile in a foreign land, her hopes and dreams had been of more grown-up and sober fare, such as freedom, safety, security, and eventually going back to the homeland. Though the Jews lived in peace and had managed to assimilate into this foreign society, they were still careful. Passionate about their heritage and their faith, they saw the invisible lines of demarcation and knew their boundaries. They never knew when the tide would turn. She was sure this was why Mordecai, her cousin and guardian, had told her not to reveal her identity. She wondered if the king would care, but she would not chance finding out. Though she was going to be queen, she still viewed Mordecai as her father. She chose to honor him as such and yield to his authority.

Though the women who were in the harem proudly stated their origins as if it were a badge of their identity, Esther kept silent on her background, making her an anomaly to the people who interacted with her. Though they speculated on her heritage based on her exotic looks, they were unable to pin her to one locale. Esther smiled and let them talk. The information they sought would not come from her lips. She knew who she was, and that was all that mattered. She was a Jewish woman God had seen fit to put into this amazing position.

Next, she wouldn't be just a queen. She would also be the wife of the king. The title "queen" was one thing, but it was only a title. It was not who she was. She was a wife, but this also didn't define her. If she were no longer a wife or a queen tomorrow, she would still be who she was. She would be no greater or no less a person of value. This she knew. She knew who she was without all the trappings and lofty station.

This knowledge kept her sober. She didn't know why she was in this position, but she trusted God would unfold all things in His timing. In the midst of all the headiness that would have affected any woman, she knew she must stay true to who she was. Some of the women had changed since becoming a part of the harem. Though some had never had servants before, they were now spoiled and temperamental, unkind and self-important. Esther saw no need to be rude and inconsiderate to her attendants. Given a set of different circumstances, she could have been one of them. Many of her fellow countrymen had been slaves and servants. But for the grace of God she wasn't. She would never take her position for granted or abuse it. She remained the gracious, thoughtful woman she had been before she entered the palace. This was the posture of a true queen.

⤿◊◊◊⤾

After speaking at a woman's conference, I was visiting with a woman who had approached me. She said, "I'm still trying to find myself. I feel as if I've lost my identity since I got married." I tried to make light of the subject to lift the cloud of heaviness from her. "What do you mean?" I asked. "How can you be looking for yourself? You're standing right here. You haven't gone anywhere!"

She chuckled, but then I grew serious. My light response had a double meaning. It was true. She wasn't as lost as she thought she was. She was right here. She just needed to locate herself back to who she was before she married her husband. What were her dreams and passions? How did she describe herself before meeting her mate? The woman she was had attracted her husband in the first place. Somewhere between the "I do's" and images of what being a wife looks like, she got lost. Distracted by trying to please her man and balancing her career and family life, some dreams were pushed to the back burner and seemingly died. Without those dreams, the feeling of going through the motions of life without the emotion of passion that fuels purpose arose.

When we know who we are, there is no need for announcements about our identity or efforts to prove it. Who we are will speak up as our purpose unfolds. When we stay true to who we are, we don't allow the changes of life or our circumstances to rearrange the priorities God has set in our hearts. We need to realize that the same things we bring to our romantic relationships are the same things that will continue to fuel it. Being authentic to who we are without announcement speaks volumes about our self-esteem and the confidence that can only come from having our identity firmly established in God within our hearts. Who we are is more than a family name, race, country of origin, financial background, marital status, or even religion. Who we are is who God created us to be! That is at the root of how we need to see ourselves and what we want others to see in us. "It's in Christ that we find out who we are and what we are living for" (Ephesians 1:11 MSG).

Based on the fact that shifting mores can make one thing or another popular, our identity has to be established in something else. The opinion of others should never be the benchmark for who we are and how acceptable or lovable we are. Our significance can never be measured by external factors or situational information. Our significance comes from how God defines us.

Perhaps Esther intuitively knew it was not her lineage that would have an impact on the king, but rather who she was to him, what she had to offer that would add value to his world. As women of God, whether single or married, we must remember that nothing will matter more to the people in our world than how we make them feel when they are with us. Do they feel significant, valued, loved, and truly heard? One of the descriptions of a good wife to be desired in the book of Proverbs is that the heart of her husband can trust in her and that he will have no lack of gain (Proverbs 31:11 NKJV). This speaks of a woman who knew how to make her man feel safe with her. He didn't live in fear of her reprisals or her lack of wisdom; rather, he saw her as an oasis in the midst of his turbulent world.

When we deal with our identity as women, we need to go back to the purpose God created us for so we'll focus on the right things. Our self-esteem isn't rooted in our feelings about ourselves. Instead, it's rooted in the anticipation of living to the fullest potential of our God-given purpose. God created us as women to add amazing dimensions to a man's world, as well as the world at large, by using the gifts He's placed within us. As the story of Esther unfolds, we'll see how all her gifts—discernment, prudence, discretion, wisdom, knowledge, and influence—worked together to make her the queen she was created to be.

Take a minute to look in a mirror. Make an honest assessment of the *internal* workings of the woman looking back at you. As you align yourself with God's original design for you, your identity is solidified and a sense of wholeness will overtake you that no one can affect. This rock-solid foundation is the passion that lies deep within. It's called destiny. It calls you, challenging you to rise to the height of your true identity as a woman of God who will contribute to the world in immeasurable ways by simply being who you were created to be.

You and I respond to the things that cause our hearts to beat with a fervor that can't be dampened. We want to make a difference wherever we can. To be fruitful and multiply the kingdom of God within our personal spheres one life at a time. As daughters of the King, the most High God, our identity begins and ends at the foot of the cross of Jesus, completely surrendered to our Creator who knows us and loves us most.

Reflections

✣ If you had to introduce or describe you, what would you say?

✣ What attributes of yours add value to the quality of your mate's life?

✣ How would your mate describe you?

Love Talk

The greatest gift you can give your mate is the certainty of who you are. Insecurity is a burden to your partner because it makes him feel responsible for things that are beyond the scope of his capabilities. No one can be responsible for your joy, peace, and sense of wholeness but you. These things are found only in the solid knowledge of who you are and whose you are.

10

Revealing the Enemy

In those days, as Mordecai was sitting at the king's gate, Bigthan and Teresh, two of the king's eunuchs, who guarded the threshold, became angry and sought to lay hands on King Ahasuerus. And this came to the knowledge of Mordecai, and he told it to Queen Esther, and Esther told the king in the name of Mordecai. When the affair was investigated and found to be so, the men were both hanged on the gallows. And it was recorded in the book of the chronicles in the presence of the king (Esther 2:21-23).

Esther shook her head as she pondered the recent events. She remembered how she first felt when Mordecai relayed the information that someone wanted to harm the king. Her cousin had been sitting at the king's gate when he overheard the whispered conversation of two of the king's eunuchs. When they aired their grievances against the king, their voices rose as they conspired on how to kill the monarch. Mordecai sat perfectly still holding his breath, careful not to draw attention to himself...even feigning being asleep. Their dissatisfaction was clear; their intentions even clearer. What had started as faint whispers had escalated to muttering in high-pitched voices that were far too audible to remain a secret as they mapped out their diabolical plan to wreak their revenge.

Upon their retreat behind the palace walls, Mordecai raised himself to his full height and contemplated the best course of action. He didn't believe God had showered Esther with the favor it takes to win the heart of a king only to be put in danger by two loose cannons. No, he must let her know about this evil plot, and she must convey it to her husband. She would know how to do it with discretion and preserve her security.

Esther remembered how her heart had beat wildly in her chest at the thought of telling her husband about this. Would he believe her? What would happen to the men? If it proved to be true what they plotted, their end would be a terrible one. She'd shaken off the possibilities for their punishment knowing it would be nothing short of death. But death by what method—that was a most disturbing thought. Yet their fate wasn't her concern. It was her husband she cared about.

Fortunately, the king sent for her the very day she received Mordecai's message. She dressed carefully that evening, making sure she was perfect for him. She'd heard he was in a foul mood, and she didn't relish the thought of adding insult to injury. Yet she must tell him. It was a matter of life or death. She weighed when would be the best time to broach the topic. After dinner would be best, when he was sure to be in better humor.

She remembered his face as the dawning of what she relayed hit him. Though controlled, his countenance was angry. She prayed she would never do anything to incur such a response. Immediately her report was investigated and found to be true. When asked how she'd come to know these things, she credited Mordecai. Yes, Mordecai had reported what he'd heard, and yes, it would be appropriate that he be rewarded for his loyalty.

Mordecai's help was recorded in the king's annals, but that was all. Esther wondered at this, and even prayerfully asked if that was enough reward for doing the right thing. Did the king think so little of life that when someone saved his, it was only worth a few words written in a book?

She and Mordecai had both done what was right, and she decided that was reward enough. Knowing they had done the right thing brought a peace that couldn't be bought. Even though she hadn't been summoned to see the king for some time now, she was grateful for the part she played in saving his life. After all, that is what a wife does with no thought of reward.

～ᴇᴇᴏ～

We all have blind spots, so we need to know someone has our backs, especially when our backs are vulnerable and threatened by enemies. Many women have a special sense of discernment about when a loved one is in danger. In the Garden of Eden, God told Adam, "Because you listened to your wife...cursed is the ground" after Adam and Eve disobeyed God and sinned (Genesis 3:17 NIV). I find that ironic because God personifies wisdom as a woman in the book of Proverbs (Proverbs 9, for example). (In all fairness, He also personifies folly as a woman.) I believe the bottom line is that a woman can be influential in a good way or a bad way. She can operate in wisdom or be the foolish woman who destroys her home with her own hands—or, far too often, with her mouth (Proverbs 14:1).

A true queen recognizes when the enemy quietly enters her man's life, and she sounds the alarm. Now, I admit that I've had people tell me the difficult truth about a person or a situation, but the manner in which they relayed the information made it hard for me to receive what they had to say. Therefore, I feel it's not enough to merely say we need to be gatekeepers in our men's lives. Much finesse must be exercised in relating information to our men.

Esther seemed to be a master at this. She exercised the height of restraint in how she shared the bad news of a murder plot with her husband. She didn't seek any credit but calmly relayed the information in such a way that she empowered her man to get to the bottom of the matter and avert disaster. (Later, Esther shows even greater restraint, but we'll get to that in another chapter.)

Of course, the enemies our men face aren't going to be two eunuchs seeking to kill them. No, in this day and age, it will probably be something much more subtle, such as a bad habit that is detrimental to their health, an area that is causing great stress that affects them negatively, or associating with someone who isn't a good influence. There are a variety of enemies and ways they can enter our men's world and threaten our security (what affects our men affects us). And sometimes we'll see the apparent danger and our men won't. And there may be times when we point out the danger, and our partners shoo the information away in the same manner as when we suggest asking for directions when they're driving. Being told about a problem often goes against the grain of a man's soul, especially when it involves an area they feel they have under control.

This is why our attitude and approach are everything. We want to empower our men to make the right decision with the information we present. This won't occur if they feel talked down to, berated, or scolded. "I told you so" moments will also fall flat. Instead, we must present the information from a place of complete devotion to their well-being so they know we aren't motivated by anything other than total regard for their welfare.

This means there is no insistence on being listened to attached to the information. No self-interest can be present in our delivery. We are simply the mail carriers delivering the mail. We are not forcing them to read it or do whatever instructions come with the letter. I find it very significant that Esther chose to divert the attention away from herself by crediting Mordecai with the finding and sending of this sensitive information. I believe this event is recorded in the Word for a reason. It shows that Esther established trust in the heart of the king. She was paying forward for a more critical time that was yet to be revealed.

Crisis has a way of building intimacy if the information and occurrence is shared in the right way. Esther exemplified the Proverbs 31 woman. The heart of her man could trust in her. She spoke the truth in love and preserved the life of her man. This is the power every wife possesses and can exercise from time to time with her king. Be careful how you wield this power!

Reflections

✻ What is your first response when you see your man in a harmful situation?

✻ How do you usually relay your observations to him? What is his typical response?

✻ How can you improve your delivery of hard truths?

Love Talk

Quiet as it's kept, the inference that man needed help went beyond his capacity to be fruitful and multiply. Woman was designed to fill gaps in the man's life. This includes moments when he doesn't see what he needs and his blind spots open him to danger. Just as other body parts quietly compensate for another part in a moment of weakness or quickly move to shield a part from hurt or danger, so a wife can care for and shield her husband. They are one flesh…one body. When she protects him, she also protects herself.

11

Understanding Your Position

*When Haman saw that Mordecai would not kneel down or pay
him honor, he was enraged. Yet having learned who Mordecai's
people were, he scorned the idea of killing only Mordecai. Instead
Haman looked for a way to destroy all Mordecai's people, the
Jews, throughout the whole kingdom of Xerxes (Esther 3:5-6).*

*[Mordecai] sent back this answer [to Esther]: "Do not think that
because you are in the king's house you alone of all the Jews will
escape. For if you remain silent at this time, relief and deliverance
for the Jews will arise from another place, but you and your
father's family will perish. And who knows but that you have
come to your royal position for such a time as this?" (4:13-14).*

Mordecai wrung his hands and paced back and forth. What had he done? Perhaps he'd been wrong to stand on principle. But at the time he didn't believe this to be so. He refused to bow to Haman or any other official in government because it went against his faith. According to God's Word, he could pay homage to no one but God. He was not to bow before humans or images of any kind. God refused to share His glory with another. Mordecai didn't speak out against the Persian gods. He was in Persia and had learned to tolerate the country's practices and beliefs. However, he was determined to not participate in their pagan practices. He didn't protest them worshipping their way, and he hoped he'd be allowed to worship as God commanded. This was only fair.

But Haman was hateful and proud—a bad combination. Mordecai had to admit that he wasn't sorry for not bowing and paying tribute to him, but he was appalled that his offense would cost people their lives. Why should all the Jews in the king's domain pay for the sin of one? Yet the die had been cast. Haman had convinced the king that the Jews were an enemy that must be extinguished.

The weight of this injustice pressed heavily on Mordecai. He had to do something! He sent a message to Esther, asking her to intercede. She must go on behalf of her people. Now was the time to reveal her background—it must be a matter of divine timing. Now was the time for her to use her position as queen to intercede for the safety of the Jews. Esther must go to the king! Mordecai could see no other solution. He prayed for the favor of God to precede her as she went to speak to the king.

And now he'd received Esther's reply. He looked at Esther's messenger, Hathak, with consternation. What did Esther mean she couldn't approach the king? He asked Hathak to repeat the message:

> All the king's servants and the people of the king's provinces
> know that if any man or woman goes to the king inside the
> inner court without being called, there is but one law—to
> be put to death, except the one to whom the king holds out
> the golden scepter so that he may live. But as for me, I have
> not been called to come in to the king these thirty days.

Obviously Esther didn't understand the gravity of the situation. Did she not realize she'd been chosen? Not just by the king, but by God? Chosen to be in the position she was in? Mordecai weighed his words before drafting a reply. Just as his one offense could cost many people their lives, Esther must be the one to bring redemption. Her position as queen meant she was the only one who could help. That she was in this position must not be taken lightly or viewed as coincidence. No, it had to be a divine mandate! The palace may be the head, but the city was the body, and everything that occurred in the palace would affect everyone within its shadow.

Mordecai needed to cut through Esther's sense of self-preservation. This was bigger than her safety. This was a matter of life and death for all the Jews in this foreign land. Didn't Esther understand what a miracle it was that she, a young woman from the Jewish nation, had been chosen to be queen of Persia? Didn't she understand this was a matter of destiny and not personal fulfillment? Mordecai decided he must call her attention to these facts immediately. Too many lives were at stake. Whether she liked it or not, everything was hanging on her choice.

◦ᴇᴇᴊᴊᴊᴊ◦

A woman has to understand that what happens at her house ultimately affects her community, state, and maybe the very world. How many times has one event that was seemingly insignificant sent shockwaves around the globe? This is a principle found in God's Word: "The body has many different parts, not just one part. If the foot says, 'I am not a part of the body because I am not a hand,' that does not make it any less a part of the body... The eye can never say to the hand, 'I don't need you'" (1 Corinthians 12:14-15,21). We are one body. What hurts one part affects every other part eventually. When we conduct ourselves with a kingdom mentality, we make different choices, realizing the effects our choices make beyond our personal space. As the saying goes, "Evil flourishes when good men or good women do nothing."

Esther had a serious problem. First, she had an enemy. Though indirect, Haman's agenda would eventually hurt her. Though her husband lived outside the realm of Haman's agenda, the annihilation of the Jews would also have a negative impact on his domain and on him personally. He would lose his wife and many people who worked in the kingdom. It would upset the economy and how the kingdom operated. King Ahasuerus had probably given little thought to the far-reaching implications of wiping out the Jews in his kingdom. Haman had done a good job of convincing him that the Jews were a threat to his safety and authority. So now Esther was being asked to take a step of faith to save her people.

How does a godly wife approach her husband? That was the question. Not only was Esther's husband an unbeliever, he was also a very powerful king. He'd proven his capacity for rash action in his dealings with Vashti. And Esther knew he had ultimate authority over her and all that pertained to her life. Yes, it was true what Mordecai said. The king had chosen her, which gave her special privilege and access, but she needed to approach him carefully. How could she best use that access?

In this sense, every woman needs to know her position and her power. If a wife is married to an unbeliever, she may feel limited in what she can do because her husband isn't operating with the same values and priorities she is. However, I believe the story of Esther brings an amazing principle to the fore. In spite of the beliefs of your husband, God can operate and give you the favor it takes to help make your concerns your man's concerns. After all, the hearts of kings are in God's hands.

You have leverage because this man chose to spend the rest of his life with you. Trust me, he wants his home filled with peace. This means he wants you happy because he knows "If mama isn't happy, nobody is happy." It's not enough to believe your mate should want to give you what you want because you're his wife. You need to help him. The Word of God invites us to cast our cares on the Lord because He cares for us. This is key. God cares for us; therefore, our cares become His cares. So you need to nurture the heart of your husband in such a way that he cares so much for you that your concerns become his. Next, your concerns need to be kingdom centered not self-centered. When your desire involves more than you, your husband will be more apt to take notice and, if needed, take measures to correct the situation. For instance, in Esther's case, though Esther and her people were threatened by Haman, the consequences would directly affect the king, his household, and his work.

Esther knew she was a wife and a queen. She had been personally chosen by the king. And she knew she was at risk from Haman's plot to kill the Jews. She also knew that she could use her influence with the king only if she proceeded in the right manner. Above all, she had to be confident that when she stepped out in faith to stand in the gap for her people God would go with her. Knowing that taking the risk wasn't for personal glory but for a higher purpose gave her courage. If that purpose wasn't fulfilled, her being queen was in vain.

Let me interject an important truth here. There are times when God might simply direct you to take action instead of intercede. When King David's men approached Nabal to ask for food, Nabal refused even though David's army had provided protection for Nabal's workers and livestock. When Nabal's wife, Abigail, was told of the situation, she stepped in and took action. "Nabal" means fool, and the man lived up to his name. He couldn't be reasoned with or prodded into doing the right thing. Therefore, Abigail had to stand in the gap for her husband. She went to the king and saved the lives not only of Nabal and herself, but of their entire staff (1 Samuel 25).

In this situation, the danger wasn't confined to Abigail's personal well-being. The problem extended to the household and workers. Abigail took action and allayed David's anger. Later, when she shared with her husband what she had done to save lives, God stepped in to take up her part. He removed Nabal, paving the way for Abigail to become a wife of King David.

Abigail's right response influenced the right people, which saved the day and put her in a position to be blessed by God and honored by King David. She put herself in harm's way by going to David on behalf of her husband because she was more concerned about the far-reaching effects of her husband's foolishness than her own safety. She dared to stand in the gap.

We women need to realize that being a wife isn't just about personal fulfillment or security. It's about helping to equip our husbands to be the men God created them to be. We want to influence their choices for the good, which will affect the world at large, decision by decision. As we examine the input of women throughout the Bible, we see a pattern. The choices their men made based on their wives' advice and presence often positively affected many others.

First, we need to pick our battles. In some instances, intercession is the better route to take, taking a stand until the situation is resolved. Then God will step in and take up our part. Next, depending on the situation, we may realize we can't afford to turn a blind eye to what our partners are doing. We must see the far-reaching effects and be willing to put ourselves on the line to speak the truth in love. Sometimes fearing their mate's wrath, women opt for silence. We don't always realize that respite from wrath doesn't guarantee we'll escape disaster. Remembering our purpose in times when our families, households, and domains might be at risk is our motivating factor for rising to the occasion and taking action.

Reflections

❧ What situations cause you to seek the intervention or help of your mate?

❧ Think of a time when you asked for his help and he didn't respond as you wanted. How did you handle it? What do you think were his reasons for not responding how you expected?

❧ What guidelines will help you discern or weigh a situation to determine whether you should approach your mate about it or take action and talk to him later?

Love Talk

A man lives to be his woman's hero. In every situation, strive to empower him to be exactly that. Let your position illuminate his, so that he will want to meet your needs. Be careful not to overshadow your king. Because you love him, you'll be passionate about preserving his well being, his kingdom, and the peace of your household. When they are secure, so are you.

12

Unwavering Faith

*Then Esther sent this reply to Mordecai: "Go, gather together all
the Jews who are in Susa, and fast for me. Do not eat or drink
for three days, night or day. I and my attendants will fast as
you do. When this is done, I will go to the king, even though it
is against the law. And if I perish, I perish" (Esther 4:15 NIV).*

 sther took a deep breath. Mordecai was right. It was by the grace
 of God that she was where she was. She'd never thought she'd be
the queen of such a mighty nation or be married to such a powerful
man. And now a weightier thought was thrust upon her. Hers was no
simple, straightforward marriage. No, it had much more significance.
As Mordecai had said, "Who knows whether you have not come to
the kingdom for such a time as this?" (Esther 4:14). Being elevated to
this position had a purpose—God's purpose. This was her destiny! She
was chosen for a far greater purpose than serving her man tea. This was
more profound than the intimacy she shared with her husband and
much deeper than the responsibility her title carried. The lives of others were in her hands. What took place within these walls would have
far-reaching effects.

She swallowed hard. The king hadn't called for her for sometime
now. She understood that the rigors of carrying out kingdom business

consumed him. Though she was queen, she didn't insist on being his first priority. Though he favored her most of all, she was but one part of his complicated world. She knew that peace would only be found in releasing him to be who he was and do what he did. That beat despairing over the parts of his life she couldn't have. But now she must go to him, summoned or not. She must exercise wisdom. This was a delicate situation that must be handled with great prudence.

She wasn't sure what she should do or how to approach her husband. She knew she had to get still before God and await His direction. This she'd learned from Mordecai, and it was perhaps the most valuable lesson she'd had. Esther sent word to her cousin asking him to have the Jews in the city join her in prayer and fasting. She would trust God to deliver clear steps for her to take. She knew the power of agreement in prayer would work on her behalf to get God's attention and open her mind to His wisdom.

Esther shut herself in her chambers, along with her maidservants, in anticipation of hearing God's voice, of receiving clarity on the path she should take. For three days she stilled the clamoring distractions and turned away from food. She depended on God for sustenance. She wanted nothing to stand between her and her heavenly Father. She needed His counsel more than ever before. She paced back and forth, clasping and unclasping her hands. Waiting…waiting…until she felt an overwhelming sense of peace and with it a sweet release of what to do.

Yes, she was ready to do God's will. She'd emptied herself of personal agendas, remaining open to what God wanted to accomplish through her. She knew what to do now, and she would move forward without fear. "If I perish, I perish" went through her mind, but she knew God's will would be done and He was with her.

～ஐ௹௹~

How many times have you feared going to your mate with a request you felt he might not see as vital as you do? The fear of rejection can be overwhelming and paralyzing. No one wants to be told that what is important to him or her isn't as important to the other person. Whether you've observed a personal issue or your spouse is doing something that might be hurtful to himself, you, your children, his career, or whatever, the truth needs to be spoken in love. But there's more to it. The truth also must be spoken at the right time. "The right word at the right time is like a custom-made piece of jewelry, and a wise friend's timely reprimand is like a gold ring slipped on your finger" (Proverbs 25:11 MSG). In other words, correction at the right time and done in the right way will help the person recognize that the shoe fits and he will gladly wear it. When spoken in the wrong way at the wrong time, more damage can be done than if nothing was said.

There have been times in my life when people spoke the truth to me, but the manner and time in which they conveyed the information overshadowed their wisdom. I rebelled by not receiving what they had to say—to my own hurt later on down the line. People can be right about situations, but they can also be sincerely wrong if they don't wisely approach the subject with the right timing and words.

A well-known adage says we should never move out of anger or fear. Both these emotions can trigger bad decisions with lasting repercussions. That's why it was so wise of Esther to take a deep breath, empty herself of her own agenda, ask for prayer and support, get before God, and then wait to hear from Him on how to deal with the situation. It was not the time to panic. It was the time to exercise wisdom tempered by discretion and prudence. God's Word tells us that wisdom will protect and guard us (Proverbs 4:6). Wisdom is accompanied by friends we all need in the midst of desperate times: knowledge, discernment, common sense, success, riches, honor, enduring wealth, and justice. With these provided through God, we have all we need to face the dilemmas of the day.

Esther needed to draw on wisdom to think through what she'd talk about with the king so she could state her case clearly. She needed discernment to know the best way to approach the king. She needed common sense so she wouldn't be so heavenly minded that she ended up being no earthly good. In other words, she needed "street sense" to approach the king where he lived and on a level that mattered to him.

Success, riches, honor (the respect of her peers), and enduring wealth all help to attain justice. Unfortunately, people tend to respond more quickly to someone who is wealthy and in a prominent position. As some say, "Money talks." Let's look at this in the spiritual and emotional sense. Think of money as the currency of investing ourselves completely in a person or situation. This must be an investment the other person can feel or we will get no return on our investment. Esther needed to get rid of her own agenda for God to fill her with all she would need as she stood before the king.

In everyday relationships, one mistake often made is that we go before a mate, spouse, friend, colleague, or child filled to the brim or overflowing with our own agendas. Uppermost in our minds is what *we* want from the person or situation instead of stopping long enough to discover what God has in mind. We rob ourselves of the positive results we long for when we do this. Instead of praying, "Lord, change this person," perhaps our prayer should be, "Lord, what do You want me to do in this scenario? What would You like to accomplish through me? How can I help Your agenda be fulfilled? And, Lord, if necessary, change me." After praying this, I'm sure our approach to the issue would be better received…and perhaps drastically different than what we'd originally desired.

Dealing with a difficult situation isn't something you have to do alone. Having an inner circle of friends who help keep you transparent and accountable goes a long way. Give these people permission to speak the truth in love to you, to correct and reprove as need be. Esther shut herself in with her maidservants, knowing she would be bolstered by their agreement in prayer and fasting together.

As I've noted, in the Bible the number seven is significant because it speaks of perfection and maturation, of something coming to the fullness of fruition. Esther was about to have a divinely inspired appointment with the king. And she wanted and needed divine intervention to guide her and give her resolve. Like the Hebrew boys Shadrach, Meshach, and Abednego, who were thrown into a fiery furnace but remained confident that no matter what the outcome, their God was with them, Esther had to be willing to move forward on the strength of her convictions even if she didn't feel God's immediate presence with her in the throne room. (For more on Shadrach, Meshach, and Abednego, read Daniel 3.) The purpose of Esther's appearance had to be greater than her fear.

Any woman who desires a better marriage, better relationships, a better home life, a better life in general has to be willing to ask the hard questions and receive, at times, the even harder answers. The spirit of fighting for the best in and from your man needs to remain at the core of all your interactions with him. The spirit of defeat must not be allowed to rise up. And the understanding that the fight might cost you everything, including your pride, your tidy demeanor, your image, and so forth in order to help you draw the best out of your man cannot be a deterrent. Therefore, all women at some point in a marriage or romantic relationship must reach a sacrificial mindset and utter Esther's famous words, "If I perish, I perish."

Reflections

❄ What is your usual mindset when you present a problem to your partner?

❄ What steps do you take to prepare for your talk with him?

❄ What attitudes or emotions do you need to get rid of or counter before approaching him?

Love Talk

"People don't care what you know. They only want to know that you care." Favor is always birthed out of a positive relationship. As you approach your man to talk about a problem or what you need, make sure pride and selfishness don't accompany you. Go alone, naked (vulnerable) and unashamed (open). In this posture your man will truly desire to help you and cover you.

Part 4

Where Is Your Power?

*M*uch has been said about the wiles and strength of a woman. But it is important to focus on the strengths that God has given to women. Yes, we can manufacture similar strengths in our flesh, but they will be mere counterfeits doing more harm than good. For example, God has given us the gift of influence, but the enemy of our souls tries to pervert this inherent part of who we are by encouraging us to be manipulative. The Bible says that manipulation is likened to the sin of witchcraft (Nahum 3:4). Witchcraft and manipulation both attempt to influence someone to do something they might not otherwise do. It is "manufactured influence," in a sense. The person is not allowed to come to his own natural conclusion. A power outside of him that is not God is at work moving him against his natural will. Usually when people come to their senses, the fallout is terrible because they feel they've been used or played. We will be looking at several "power conductors," if you will, in this next section after taking a brief overview of the areas we'll be looking into more deeply.

So how do we become women who are aware of our power and use it wisely for positive, lasting, and godly outcomes? Esther exemplifies a woman of power in this sense. We see that first of all she was a woman set apart. That which is common will never be powerful. The rare finds in life make the most profound statements. When we find special things that we acquire, we place them in special places because we recognize their worth. As we look at institutions around the world that are influential in trends, a common trait is they have managed to set themselves apart. They are distinct and recognized to be so by their patrons and onlookers. They don't run with the pack. They have reserved themselves to focus on one area and excel.

As a woman, your power is also found in being distinct. Billy Joel wrote a song years ago about a woman having "a way about her." He didn't quite know what it was that got him all turned around, but her uniqueness was her power, her allure, that made her stay on his mind. So many television shows these days seem to aim to make women common, stripping them of their feminine allure. And yet being feminine—being a woman who makes no apologies for her gender—is one of the things a man finds most intriguing. If he wants male companionship, he can find someone to hang out with. But there's something about a woman! The world has taken great pains to dummy down the value of women and even denigrate the mystique about us that makes us so powerful. Media tries to reduce us to shrews—sneaky, vindictive females who can't be trusted. And yet one of the most powerful things about a woman in love is her commitment to being in her man's corner and shielding his heart, his dreams, and his secrets.

A woman will also be as powerful as the company she keeps. The Word of God tells us that bad company corrupts good character (1 Corinthians 15:33 NIV). That is true. As we walk with people, we tend to absorb their mindsets or attitudes, and that can be good or bad. Let's say you hang out with people who are movers and shakers. They are going places. They are full of new ideas, enthusiasm, and ways to make money and contribute to the world. Well, guess what you're going to think about? Yes! The same things. We absorb our personal culture from those we spend the most time with. Research has shown that we are like our three closest friends. Doesn't that mirror the adage that birds of a feather flock together? Amos 3:3 (NKJV) says, "Can two walk together unless they are agreed?"

Many married women get into trouble because they still want to behave as if they are single. I've always found it a little sad when someone gets married and their friends change, but in a way I understand why. If the rest of the newly married woman's friends are single and envious, they may not respect her relationship or they may advise her wrongly in the times she confides about issues she may be having with her spouse. To have a successful marriage, it's best to take counsel from those who are in successful marriages or those who, though single, are completely grounded in God's views on marriage and womanhood. Otherwise you may be in a situation where the blind is leading the blind.

Of course, prayer is the foundation of a woman's power. Her communion with God is the gateway to wisdom and divine intervention. Not every issue in your romantic relationship will be something you can master in the natural. There will be times when the Spirit of God will have to deal with your man. This is the point when it's tempting to manipulate. However, you don't want to settle for a temporary fix. You want lasting results, and they only come from changed hearts. And only God can truly change a heart.

We have open access to God at all times! We need to take our relationship concerns to Him. We need to seek His face and get the answers for our relationships to thrive and have fruitful outcomes. God is faithful that way. He has a tender heart toward His women. He is also aware of the power He has deposited in us. He guards jealously over us to protect us from the influence of the enemy, who would love to get us to mishandle our gifts. Prayer keeps us focused on dealing with our desires and situations God's way. Being still before God silences our clamoring insistences and calms us so we can hear His gentle whisper that always offers real solutions.

Finally, and I'm sure I've said it a thousand times, *attitude is everything*. If you say the right thing the right way, you will get much further than if you say the right thing the wrong way. We all know that out of the abundance of the heart the mouth speaks (Matthew 12:34). Therefore, we must do the head work and heart work it takes to control our countenances and our tongues when we approach our loved ones. Inevitably, if we are filled with angry thoughts, we will utter angry words.

When we know that God is backing us up in our concerns and the things we would like to present as needs to our mates, we can calmly and lovingly present them in a way that won't come off as demanding. When we inspire our men to address our concerns, they'll always do so far better than if they feel coerced.

Last, but not least, our personal presentation can be very powerful. After all, we captured our partners' attention before we captured their hearts. The temptation to relax after we've "closed the deal" can be the undoing of many a relationship. Not only do we have to do the work it takes to keep our heads and our hearts together, we need to do what it takes to keep our bodies and appearance together as well. This means taking care of ourselves from the inside out.

And friends, insecurity can make us say things that will call attention to aspects our partners may never notice until we bring them up. For instance, your mate might think you are looking fine…until you mention that you need to lose weight. Now that's what's on his mind when he looks at you. This is why we must be still before our heavenly Father and allow Him to build our esteem in Him. As we look into His Word and commune before Him, He gives us His picture of who we are. As we embrace His image of us and His design for our lives, we are able to walk in confidence while continuing to strive to be all He wants us to be.

When a man likes what he sees, he will do what he needs to do to have access to that vision. Your appearance should give him pleasure. It should be a welcome distraction from the mundane aspects of his day. We should never relax when it comes to our appearance. The wow factor is something we need to maintain to the best of our ability. As time goes by and age and other life changes take their toll, it's natural and inevitable that we will not look the same as we once did.

But we need to work toward being the best we can be in every season of our lives.

Does your man see the effort you put into being your best and know it's for both of you? Let's face it. When we know we're looking good, our confidence is boosted. And a confident woman is a powerful woman.

13

Set Apart

Then Esther told them to reply to Mordecai, "Go, gather all the Jews to be found in Susa, and hold a fast on my behalf, and do not eat or drink for three days, night or day" (Esther 4:15).

Esther closed the doors behind her and took a deep breath. She had committed to going to the king. She knew she needed to prepare her heart and mind before she went. She paced back and forth as she considered the situation. She needed to still her pounding heart and silence the fears that were screaming in her mind. Now was not the time to listen to various opinions on how to deal with this dilemma. This would be between the king and her. She knew a word to the wrong person could start a fire that might not be extinguishable. She also knew the power of the rumor mill within the palace. There were too many people with far too much time on their hands, too many people jockeying for favor with the king. Any sign of weakness or indiscretion exposed was often used to discredit and remove the unfortunate and unsuspecting from the court. For this reason, the wise person knew to exercise the greatest discretion at all times.

From almost the time Esther had arrived at the court she'd been set apart from the crowd. Hegai had taken special pains to give Esther her own apartments in the choicest section of the harem. She'd not been privy to the daily goings on around her. Hegai had kept her well shielded from them on purpose, knowing the mayhem that could ensue should the wrong word be said or the right word misinterpreted. No, Esther had stayed well above the fray, and she preferred it that way.

And now she was a married woman and the queen! She had her own apartments within the palace. She was well aware that her personal business should be kept private. She sought to cover her man, not expose him. She knew that at every opportunity people all around sought information about the king to use for their personal gain. She also knew it was easy to slip into conversations about her husband and not be aware how an innocent comment she said about him could be elaborated on or blown up into something it wasn't.

No, it was better to walk softly and avoid any potential pitfalls when it came to rubbing elbows with those who dwelt within the palace walls. She wanted no part of intrigue, and she was quite happy to confine herself to her apartments until the king called for her. When he didn't call, she found other ways to busy herself that kept her away from idle minds and busy tongues that might create mayhem or even evil with their chatter. There was safety in keeping her circle small and staying in control of her personal space. She lived to please God and her husband—and few others.

Esther didn't feel isolated. She chose to think of herself as consecrated. She recognized the profound import of her position and didn't take it for granted. After all, Vashti, the queen before her, hadn't exercised prudence and had been replaced. Esther would not offer a repeat performance of what had occurred before.

Right now the time was more critical than ever. She needed to hear from God on this matter of life and death before she proceeded. She didn't want advice or counsel from people with hidden agendas or selfish motives. She needed clarity and wisdom. This she could only get from one source—the one who sat on a throne greater than that of her husband. All other voices must be silenced, including her own. She wanted to hear God's voice alone. She took another deep breath as she closed the doors to her bedroom chamber. Here she could pray in peace, completely set apart from the palace staff. Here she could give God her full attention. She sat quietly, meditatively, and waited.

❧❧❧❧❧

There comes a time in the life of every woman when she comes to the place of knowing when to separate herself from others for the sake of her love relationship. This is called maturing into her position as a woman committed to a person or cause. A famous commercial noted that "what happens in Vegas stays in Vegas." The same must be true of our relationships with our men. What a man hates most is being uncovered to our friends and family. Remember the proverb that says, "The heart of her husband trusts in her"? A man wants to know that what happens in his home between his wife and him remains there. (However, in cases of violence or abuse, please don't hesitate to ask for advice and take action to keep everyone safe.)

When conflict arises, so does the temptation to talk to as many people as possible to get support and have them weigh in on how the situation should be handled. This is seldom a good thing. Though it is true that there is safety in a multitude of counsel, that counsel needs to be chosen with great discretion when it comes to our love relationships. It must be done in a way that will not threaten the security of our men's hearts.

A Few Important Steps

Before presenting issues to our men, there are a few steps that are important to take. We need to set ourselves apart and be still. In our stillness with God, He will make clear what we need to know. Separation is critical to intimacy with God. This intimacy time allows Him to impart His wisdom and guidance that will lead to beneficial changes in our lives. These changes begin in our hearts and minds before they manifest in our lives.

Sometimes we need to take the time to silence the clamor of our hearts and the rationalizations of our minds before we can hear God clearly and see the situation we're dealing with realistically. Then we can make the right assessments and critical insights into how to best deal with the circumstances. It is in this "set apart time" that God is able to help us lift and separate fact from fiction, highlight what is truly important, and do away with all that is mere distraction from the real point. Only then can we have the clarity and grace we need to effectively deal with our partners. Whether it's a conflict we want resolved or a change we want to take place in our relationships, preparation must be done within so our requests will be considered.

What we're doing is preparing our hearts before we deal with our partners' hearts. By focusing on what we want and then checking to see what God wants out of our situation, we're establishing our mindset and determining what our steps and words will be. In some instances, a relationship is like a business transaction. The client has to be happy before we will be rewarded with his or her favor. When readying ourselves to make a request, it helps to be as blameless as possible so that our shortcomings don't become distractions in the midst of negotiation. Being clear about what we want and why we want it are important so we won't be swayed from our goal.

We also need to be clear as to how our men can help us. Let's face the truth. In most cases, if our partners knew what we wanted or needed, they would have taken care of it already. Often when there is an issue with us, the men in our lives are unaware of what we want, of what we are struggling with, or of how what they're doing or have done has really affected us. They won't know until we tell them. Most men aren't prophetic and don't possess ESP.

Men need things spelled out. And they appreciate it when we lovingly do that. Their nature to fix things kicks in big time when they know what to do. They are off to follow our instructions and get 'er done! They feel helpless when they don't know how to fulfill our needs because they live to be our kings and the fixers of our world.

As we keep this in mind, we need to remember to avoid the temptation to involve others in our personal business. Be set apart. This is called "sanctifying" our relationships to keep them safe. It is truly "the little foxes" and extraneous voices that can spoil the vine of love.

In critical situations, we need to pull away from others to pray and fast. We want to cleanse our minds, our hearts, and our spirits to hear clearly from God. We need to kill our flesh (self-interest) and all of its inclinations so that we can walk in the Holy Spirit. God wants to partner with us in our relational issues, but He will not shout above the voices of others or compete for our attention. When we pull apart and draw near to Him, He will do the work in our heart to prepare us for fruitful exchanges with our mates. Yes, it is in the alone place that He prepares us best for greater intimacy and stronger ties that will help bind our relationships together.

Reflections

✻ When dealing with critical issues with your man, what is your usual procedure? How has this affected your relationship in the past?

✻ Who do you seek counsel from when you have a concern about your mate or your romantic relationship?

✻ If needed, what can you do differently to change the results you usually get when confronting your partner?

Love Talk

After God, you want your man to know he is the most important person in your life. He is your conspiratorial best friend. This bond will be violated if other people are brought into your relationship issues without prior agreement. Men are not wired for exposure or confrontation; therefore, you must make sure the heart of your man feels safe before you can effectively approach him with things that are troubling you. Let him know he is your hero and not your enemy. If you bring up an issue and mention that you've discussed this with others and they support you, he'll feel the need to defend himself rather than hear what you have to say. Instead, let your quiet spirit open the door for intimate fellowship that can bring about the healthy results you desire.

14

The Company You Keep

*I and my young women will also fast as you
do. Then I will go to the king (Esther 4:16).*

Esther arose and went into her sitting room. She called her hand-maidens and bade them to sit down. Then she sat and looked at them. They were beautiful, but that wasn't what impressed her. They'd been with her for some time now. Hegai had handpicked them to attend her when she'd arrived at the palace. At first they had observed each other wordlessly, sizing each other up. The women had served Esther without complaint, neither being too standoffish nor too committed lest she not be chosen as queen. They didn't want to get attached until the outcome of this beauty contest had been decided. They might be sent off to serve a different woman, and that would be harder to do if they were emotionally invested in Esther.

Then Esther had been chosen queen. The women had been genuinely happy for her. Although she could have chosen her own servants at that point, Esther kept the seven Hegai had chosen. They attended to her every need and coached her on the things they knew about the king and the court. They proved loyal, and not just loyal but also of like minds. *How had Hegai known?* Esther wondered. She nodded her head. He'd proven to be more and more discerning by the day. Even now he stood by to make sure she was being served well and to offer his advice. Hegai and her maids were valuable allies in the court. But the maidservants were her inner circle, her confidantes. They kept her secrets, and, most importantly, they were her prayer partners. Her undergirding intercessors who were ready and willing to pray with her through any situation.

The seven women were stable and older than Esther. They were wise in the ways of womanhood and the palace. Gently they guided her and taught her how to love her husband. There were no hidden agendas and selfish motives at play. They had become a sisterhood celebrating one another's victories and cheering each other on. They wept when one of them wept and shared the gift of laughter among themselves in times of great cheer. They understood the inner workings of the palace. They knew the spiritual climate of the culture, but they shared her sensitivity to God. When Esther called them and asked them to join her in prayer and fasting, they willingly responded. Esther knew the power of agreeing before God. These women would be her lifeline while she literally took her life into her hands and went before the king.

Quietly she shared why she needed their support. There was a situation of a critical nature. She needed clarity and strength from God. She needed His favor and guidance because she needed to urgently see the king.

The servants' eyes widened. They knew Esther hadn't been sent for. They knew the penalty for appearing before the king without being summoned. They agreed to fast and pray with her. They would wait on God together.

∽ฅฅฅ∾

Many a marriage has been ruined by friends giving the wrong advice and suggestions. Perhaps this is why Paul encouraged the older women to be "quiet and respectful in everything they do" so they can teach "the younger women to live quietly, to love their husbands and their children, and to be sensible and clean minded, spending their time in their own homes, being kind and obedient to their husbands so that the Christian faith can't be spoken against by those who know them" (Titus 2:3-5 TLB). That is a long laundry list, but we can be successful with God's help and be good role models who are willing to share our trade secrets on relationships.

What is even more powerful than one woman is a group of women banded together supporting and empowering one another to meet the demands of their individual worlds. What a married woman doesn't need is a bunch of unhappy single women who neither respect her marriage nor know what to do to keep a marriage strong. Now, I'm not saying that married women can't have single friends. What I am saying is that a married woman must remember at all times that she is married and conduct herself accordingly. She needs to have friends who are spiritually healthy and grounded singles or who have good marriages based on God's Word because she is taking different things into consideration now that she's married. If she heeds the advice of a single woman who isn't understanding or honoring of her role as a wife, she may get into trouble. No husband likes being put in the position of feeling that your friends are interfering with your marriage. Neither is it good for them to be tempted by any of your friends.

True friends, married or single, stand with you in agreement for your marriage. They labor with you in prayer over issues and concerns. They intercede for you and encourage you to good works in your romantic relationship. They add to and support your commitment to your partner.

The power of agreement among friends is powerful. This is why you need to choose carefully the women you want to confide in. There is a reason "birds of a feather flock together." The air stream created by the birds flying in front of a flock makes it easier for the rest of the birds to follow and go in the right direction. The stream of words that issue from friends and influencers can encourage you to build a healthy marriage or put you on a path of destruction. God's Word says that a wise woman builds her house, but a foolish woman destroys her home with her own hands (Proverbs 14:1). It's fair to say that the words of those who speak into a woman's life can also build up or tear down.

The only way any of us can be consistent in speaking life into our

situations is to be consistent in prayer—the type of prayer that emp-
ties us of ourselves and fills us with what God has to say. To have friends
that will pray with us is a great blessing when we face critical times in
our lives.

Jesus told His disciples that some breakthroughs only come through
fasting and prayer (Mark 9:29 NKJV). Fasting separates the faithful
from the inconsistent. Esther knew she couldn't go before the king
in her own strength. She needed help and clarity from God and God
alone. She also wanted the support of her inner circle to still her spirit
from racing faster than her heart, to quiet her soul, and to cast down
any human rationalizations to make room for divine wisdom.

I believe Jesus was careful to take only those "who were with him"
when He went to raise a girl from the dead (Mark 5:37-43). He knew
he had to walk with those who would be in agreement with Him to
charge the atmosphere with healing power. On other occasions He
shook the dust of a town off His feet and left without doing many miracles because of the people's unbelief (Mark 6:6). Though He was full
of faith, perhaps the unbelief of others rendered the atmosphere non-
conducive for miracles. It is not that God needs our faith to perform.
We need faith to cooperate with God by utilizing what He makes available to us in order to be blessed (Mark 6:6).

The company you keep will impact your marriage. Their advice to
you in times of conflict will affect your attitude, your words, and your
ability and willingness to solve conflicts with your mate. Though God's
Word says there is wisdom in a multitude of counsel, that also means it
must be *wise* counsel. God-fearing, marriage-honoring counsel. Counsel that takes no sides but what the Word of God says about how people
are to conduct themselves.

Esther knew that peace can't be sustained or conflicts solved without prayer. Being sensitive in the spirit means you know when to turn
down your plate and turn your gaze up to the only one who holds the
key to reconciling relationship issues. Though no woman should walk
alone, you need to make sure you're walking with wise friends who
consult God before offering advice and suggestions to help equip you
to be your best in all aspects of life, including romance.

Reflections

✗ How does your husband feel about your friends?

✗ In what ways do your friends influence your interactions with your husband?

✗ In what ways do your friends support you spiritually? How do they hold you accountable?

Love Talk

The greatest weapon a woman has is prayer. Talking to God is your best avenue before, during, and after others have had their say. As you seek the face of God and get His counsel, you can rest assured that you have the greatest advocate standing with you. As long as you approach your marriage partner emptied of yourself and open to what God wants to accomplish between the two of you, you will be victorious.

15

Dressed for the Part

*On the third day Esther put on her royal robes and stood in the
inner court of the king's palace, in front of the king's quarters, while
the king was sitting on his royal throne inside the throne room
opposite the entrance to the palace. And when the king saw Queen
Esther standing in the court, she won favor in his sight, and he held
out to Esther the golden scepter that was in his hand (Esther 5:1-2).*

Esther stood and stared at her closet as she contemplated what she
should wear. She smiled when she recalled another day just as critical as this one when she had to decide what to wear. She remembered
how nervous she'd been, so unsure of herself. She'd seen some of the
outfits the other young women had selected to wear when they were
called in to see the king. She knew those garments wouldn't reflect who
she was. She could never feel comfortable wearing what they had worn.
She understood the need to be provocative enough to catch the king's
eye, but she refused to go overboard in the process. She didn't want to
be selected for what she wore. She wanted to be selected for who she
was. She knew that clothes do not the woman make.

Hegai was there to offer counsel on the most tasteful things to wear.
He supervised her hairdresser and everything concerned with her out-
ward appearance. And, if she did say so herself, he had prepared her to

perfection. She looked like a queen even though she was not yet the king's choice. Her clothes were simple with nothing to distract the king's eye away from her beauty. Soft and feminine, the lines also spoke of quality that made her bearing appear regal.

She remembered how everyone had oohed and aahed as she'd made her way down the long, winding corridor to the king's private chambers that first time so long ago. She'd kept her gaze straight ahead, fearing that if she turned she might rearrange something. Then she paused and took a deep breathe before she entered the king's foyer. When he turned to look at her, the look on his face said it all. She looked beautiful.

Now Esther wanted to achieve that same kind of perfection again. She needed that same look to come into her husband's eyes when he saw her. She knew creating a positive image to capture his eyes before she appealed to his heart would help. Esther knew her husband loved all things beautiful. His mood could be affected by the surrounding aesthetics.

The king always told Esther how beautiful she was, and yet she never took it for granted. There would always be other women vying for his attention, so she strove to put her best foot forward to keep his attention and downplay other feminine distractions.

Though she was queen, she never forgot Vashti's fate. Esther would not be guilty of the mistakes of her predecessor. She would not assume she couldn't be replaced. Hegai had taught her well. She'd developed quite the discerning eye for fashion. Now facing her wardrobe, she pondered the effect she wanted to create. Seductive but not too much that she couldn't get him to focus on the matter at hand. Just enough appeal to create in him a desire to please her. She stifled a giggle. She knew just the dress! Oh yes! She was sure to distract him away from affairs of state with that one. She eagerly pointed to her selection and turned her attention to the rest of her toilette while her servants got the dress and other necessary garments and jewelry ready.

~eeQQe~

Yes, it's true that men are visual creatures. They are very much moved by what they see. Wise women know what signals her apparel is sending. I had a friend who always dressed in a very revealing and seductive manner. Her clothes exaggerated her physical attributes, which needed no exaggeration, so the look wasn't very flattering. She would always get angry when men made what she deemed inappropriate moves toward her. On one occasion I shared with her the messages her clothing was sending, but to no avail. She felt she should be able to expose her wares if she wished, and the men should know to keep their hands off. That is true in theory. In reality, many men view such a blatant show as an invitation to touch and a promise for more.

An insecure woman who doesn't trust her natural allure to appeal to her man feels the need to rely on provocative clothing. It's like an aspiring singer who can't carry a tune. Her manager fills the stage with dancers to distract the audience from the fact that the singer's voice can't carry the weight of the concert. The audience is so wowed by the visuals and bedazzled by the experience that they fail to notice the singer can't really sing. The same is true with women and clothing. A woman's attire can sway a man's attention so he doesn't realize at first that the woman has very little to offer other than external excitement.

Many fashion magazines have done articles showing women in various fashion profiles. Then they asked men to select which woman they would want to date or to rate what type of woman she was based on her outfit. Amazingly, it wasn't the deep, plunging necklines or the miniskirts that got their attention the most. It was the simple, nicely cut dress that accentuated her curves without exaggerating any one feature. The woman wearing the nicely cut jeans with a great blouse. The one with minimal makeup and a clean and simple hairdo. These are the women they deemed themselves more comfortable to be with. This type of attire seemed to make them believe these were women they'd like to spend time with. They said, "She looks like she's fun, spontaneous, and caring." They believed these were women they could trust to take out and not be embarrassed by her getting undue attention. They thought these women would only care about receiving their attention. Very interesting!

Remember what you wore on your first official, formal date? Or, if you're married, the beautiful wedding dress you wore? Just because you've closed the deal doesn't mean you shouldn't continue to care about your appearance. Yes, a woman's work is never done. In most cases women go to work, go home to household chores, and have children who demand her attention. That's a lot! And yet we also have partners who require our attention on top of everything else. And, unfortunately, their world is filled with visual stimulation—a point we can't afford to overlook.

Let me encourage you to look your best. That includes taking the time to have an exercise regime that keeps you healthy and in shape, no matter how much you hate it. Physical appearance and fitness is important for keeping passion alive in your relationship, as well as generating good feelings because you know you look your best. Yes, I believe it's true. You can only love your husband as much as you love and take care of yourself. Your husband will love you only as much as you love yourself. If you're not comfortable in the skin you're in, your interactions and intimacy with him will be affected.

Another thing to keep in mind is that your appearance reflects his care for you. The woman is the glory of the man. That glory reflects his presence in your life, his power, his fulfillment of his role as a husband to cover, protect, and provide for you. Your looking good tells the world he is doing a good job as a husband.

How many times have girlfriends gathered to assess an engagement ring of a friend and uttered, "Ooh, he did good!" Why? Because her man selected a great ring that reflected not just his great taste but also his investment in the relationship. Likewise, when we glorify God, our lives become testimonies of His goodness. We are letting the world know that He is a good provider. We are speaking of His goodness and faithfulness to those who believe in Him. First comes the natural, and then comes the spiritual.

Your beauty and the fact that you went to all the effort to look your best for your man will gain you serious deposits in your love bank. Learn to read your man and note what he responds to. If he likes you in red, wear plenty of it. How you look, feel, and smell are things that linger on his mind. They make him come home early instead of hanging out with his friends. Keeping your love fresh by making him feel special because you still dress to please him will touch his heart and put him in a receptive mood for pleasing you.

Men are competitive in nature, so the more you bless him, the more he will want to reciprocate. And keep in mind that the secretary and women he works with and interacts with are taking the time to look their best before going to work. Don't let your man come home and find you looking less than your best, especially if you take the time to put on your best for work. That would be like giving him leftovers, and very few people want that.

Esther knew that if she wanted her man to be receptive to her request, she needed to warm his heart by reminding him of why he'd chosen her for his queen. Although the king hadn't summoned her, Esther realized that by looking her best she would remind him how much he desired her and wanted to please her. The book of Esther tells us that it took only one glance at Esther standing just outside the throne room to make the king invite her to come closer. Clothes do not make the woman, but they do make a statement—a statement that reflects the woman within.

Reflections

✻ In what ways can you take better care of yourself physically?

✻ In what ways have you grown lax when it comes to how you look for your man?

✻ What can you do to spice up your appearance? What effect do you think this might have on your relationship?

Love Talk

What you wear on the outside is one part of your appearance. Make sure that inside you are just as beautiful. Dress your spirit as well as

your physique. The Word of God talks about the "garment of praise."
This will beautify a woman in a way that no makeup or clothing can.
A beautiful attitude is like a garment. Clothes can either complement
your beauty or make you look unattractive. Beauty starts from within,
so dress from the inside out.

16

The Right Approach

Esther approached and touched the tip of the scepter. And the king said to her, "What is it, Queen Esther? What is your request? It shall be given you, even to the half of my kingdom." And Esther said, "If it please the king, let the king and Haman come today to a feast that I have prepared for the king" (Esther 5: 2-4).

Esther held her breath as she waited for her husband to turn from those in the court and notice her. She wasn't sure what his reaction would be, yet she felt surrounded by a peaceful calm. It seemed an eternity before his gaze found her.

A flicker of pleasure grew to unmasked delight as he beckoned her forward. Lovingly he extended his scepter toward her in a show of a welcome and giving his blessing.

Joy flooded her heart. This was better than she'd hoped for. Time stood still as she walked toward him. Ever so lightly she brushed the tip of his scepter. It was cool to the touch. She looked into his eyes. Scanning his face, she tried to read what he was thinking. And then he smiled the most glorious smile. His eyes were kind and warm. The last vestiges of her reservations were dispelled.

She almost laughed at the thought of how her anxiety had played games with her. Would he be displeased that she dared enter his presence without being invited? Would he brusquely ask her to state her business and then wave her away? Or worse yet, would he order her put to death for her insolence on approaching him without being summoned? She'd heard stories of how he could be. Her mind had played a million games, all telling her it was futile to go to him. That her words would be worthless. That she was just a woman, and he would wave her away and tell her kingdom matters were above her head. What did she know about things of state and how to run a government? She knew she would stand on shaky ground, but she believed God would help her. She trusted the One who was truly sovereign and would prepare her way. And now the king—her husband—was speaking.

"What do you want, Queen Esther? What is your request? I will give it to you, even if it is half the kingdom!" (Esther 5:3 NLT).

This was music to Esther's ears, and yet she hesitated. Her eyes scanned the room. Though everyone acted like they were attending to different matters, Esther knew the people were listening closely, probably hoping for some tidbit of information to inject into the rumor mill. No, this was neither the time nor the place. She didn't want to put him on the spot. It wouldn't be good to put him into a position where he might feel the need to defend himself. Now that she had his attention, keeping the right kind of focus was critical. She looked up at him. He was waiting expectantly for her answer while she weighed her options. She'd not seen him for a while. It didn't seem right to rush into dropping a problem in his lap. Perhaps it would be best discussed over dinner, when he was full and satisfied. Yes, that was it. She would simply invite him to dinner. That was when it struck her that probably everyone in the room was there with a request. She alone was going to offer the king something personal, was going to seek his pleasure instead of asking for anything. Before she knew it, Esther thought of including Haman in the invitation. Perhaps it was best to keep her enemies close while she bought time, she thought. After all, nothing was going to happen overnight. "If it please the king, let the king and Haman come today to a banquet I have prepared for the king," Esther said.

The king beamed with pleasure, and Esther knew immediately she'd made the right choice. As she headed back to prepare for the evening, she thanked God for His divine direction and whispered a prayer for favor and for His perfect will to unfold.

ᕫᕬᕫᕬᕫ

"He who speaks first loses the deal." A woman who can master the art of restraint will see more of her desires realized. Many a relationship has been ruined by our need to prove ourselves right or to prove that we're not fools. We've got to know the right way to approach our men. This requires not only prayer and discernment, but also sensitivity to his moods, his needs, and the right timing.

I've always thought that Esther was a better woman than I am. If my man offered me up to half his kingdom, I'm sure I would come up with a long list of stuff I wanted. I'd probably even ask him to throw in a little country home far beyond the fray just for good measure.

But not Esther. She was quite focused about why she was there. She wasn't easily tempted by fare that would have more than pleased her flesh. She had an understanding of her destiny and also understood the urgency of the situation for her people. Even if there was a glimmer of possibility that she could save herself more easily than speaking for all the Jews in the kingdom, this temptation wasn't enough to deter her. Yet even with all this pressure, Esther had the presence of mind and wisdom to know that the throne room wasn't the place for her conversation with the king. No, she needed to spend time with him, make sure he was in a good mood before she made her significant request. If she was found wanting, he might not be so inclined to grant her desire. She was asking him to overturn an edict he'd authorized, after all.

Esther's restraint provides rich lessons for us. When we have needs that overwhelm us, let us "slow our roll." We want to take time to feel the temperature of the atmosphere and sense our men's hearts before proceeding. Esther was so wise! What else can we learn from her?

Never confront your man in front of other people. Intimacy breeds revelation, and revelation births change. We want to set a positive tone to establish the best possible atmosphere to get our men to listen to us with open hearts. We want to nurture intimacy, to help our men feel close to us so their deep feelings of love and protection are touched. Telling our men what we desire in front of others puts him on the spot, and most of time this will result in a negative response. He wants to maintain a certain posture or image in front of other people. Depending on the issue, he may feel he needs to defend himself if he's embarrassed or feels he's looking like he's not taking care of business. This is huge, ladies. Putting our men on the spot is not the way to go.

Next, *we want to make helping us something our men want to do.* We can do this by making sure we're meeting his needs first. We don't want them distracted by what we haven't been doing for them. The devil is in the details, and he is always ready to bring up our shortcomings to deflect us and our partners from the real issues. We may have valid points, but if our men have a list of grievances against us, our requests will be drowned out by them. Therefore, we want to make sure that all bridges are intact between our men and us before we go presenting our case, no matter what it is. "A brother offended is more unyielding than a strong city" (Proverbs 18:19). So let's make sure we're approaching happy men and not disgruntled ones.

We also want to be careful how we deal with matters concerning our men's friends or activities they enjoy that we don't like or approve of. Esther shows great finesse in this area. She didn't like Haman, but Haman was her husband's friend so she included him. Perhaps she decided to do that so when she presented her case against him to her husband, the king would know it was done from an objective light and not an emotional one. This is critical. Men do not respond well to emotion. They tend to be bottom-line people. They need to see how what is upsetting us is critical to the well-being of one or both of us in real, concrete terms.

These three elements can't be mastered until we are women under submission to God, who is able to keep us in extreme conditions and encourage us to cast all our cares on Him because we know He cares for us. This trust that God ultimately will take our part because we are blameless before Him will help us pace ourselves and approach the situation with the best attitude for success. We don't want to make demands; instead, we want to sweetly serve our men so they will choose to become the men God wants them to be, which includes caring for and watching over us.

Reflections

❧ When your needs are urgent, what is your first action to bringing it up to your mate? What are the usual outcomes of your interactions?

❧ How can you improve your approach so your mate will really hear you?

❧ In what ways can you set the tone or atmosphere to help your mate be more open to fulfilling your needs?

Love Talk

Setting the atmosphere or tone may be as simple as making your home and your arms an oasis for your man. Setting the table, making him feel special by serving him his favorite foods, letting him know how much you appreciate and love him. You can rekindle the fires you first had by doing what you did to grab and keep his attention in the first place. It's easy to settle into routine in a long-term relationship or marriage and lose the passion you had at first.

You want to pay attention to keeping love alive and strong. The world is full of temptation (for men and women). Stay sensitive and attentive. It's the little details that can harm a relationship. I encourage you to build your man up, and watch him strive to create a haven for you. The more you do to help him feel like a king, the more he will want to do to treat you like a queen. You can empower your man to do his best for you simply by making sure his needs are met first.

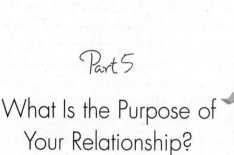

Part 5

What Is the Purpose of
Your Relationship?

M any women long to get married today. And as many as there are who long to be married, there are just as many different reasons why. Some want to be married because they feel it will validate who they are. Peer pressure says that if a woman isn't married by a certain age, something is very wrong with her. Others have been groomed their whole lives to be married. They dream of a knight in shining armor coming to carry them away to a place where they will be complete, validated, and live happily ever after. Some women want to marry for security. They want to find sugar daddies who are so wealthy they'll never have to worry about finances. Others marry because the chemistry and intimacy is so charged between them and their partners that they decide they must be together! Political alliances have been formed through marriages. Then there are arranged marriages, as is the custom in some countries, where spouses are chosen by the family to ensure that those of the same class and values are coupled, thus ensuring a union that will last.

Yes, there is a plethora of reasons that humanity seeks to join themselves together, but if we never understand why *God* put people together, we will develop the wrong expectations of what our unions should produce.

So many couples today dissolve their marriages on the simple premise that they are no longer happy. I doubt very seriously if happiness was ever one of the foundational reasons God put Adam and Eve together. Joy and happiness were by-products of them aligning themselves together for God's purposes. Joy was not the goal; fulfilling their purpose was, and in fulfilling that purpose they experienced joy.

When God said it was not good for Adam to be alone, I believe He had given Adam an assignment it would be impossible for him to complete without the help of a woman. There was no way he could be fruitful on his own. He needed the woman to partner with him in being productive and fruitful—not just in the fruit of the womb but in all the things he set his hand to do. He needed the woman to multiply. It was an assignment given to man and woman, a mandate that required them to be together to fulfill. Neither one of them could be fruitful on their own.

I find it interesting that when God chose to reserve life during the time of Noah, he commanded Noah to take at least two of every animal onto the ark two by two, male and female. It would take the male and female of a species to couple together to reproduce, to be fruitful. The two complete the puzzle it takes to reproduce. As a preacher once said, "If both of you are just alike, one of you is unnecessary."

Fruitfulness was not an option. It was a command for the man to fulfill. He was to be fruitful and multiply, to fill the earth. Adam wasn't to fill the earth with duplicates of himself; he was to fill the earth with righteous people brought up in the fear of the Lord. The earth is the Lord's. He wants to fill it with men and women who strive to look, think, walk, and talk like Him. He wants His glory reflected in the earth through His people…the people He created to have fellowship with and to serve Him. God wanted the fullness of heaven to be experienced on earth.

The strength of numbers leads to dominion. God charged the man to have dominion over and subdue every living thing. Agendas are won in the world by the sheer force of numbers backing them. A group of people represent a segment of the economy. Decisions are made on the basis of how profitable the bottom line will be. When we understand this, groups are formed and come to power through organization and the wealth they represent, not necessarily on the values of that group. God's intention was for His people to be the majority on the earth because He knows the majority rules. Based on this knowledge, God told Abraham his descendants would be as numerous as the stars in the sky.

Solomon wrote that two are better than one because they have a good reward for their labor, and if one fell down the other would be there to help him back up (Ecclesiastes 4:9-10). When a woman finds a godly partner, she has someone of like mind and spirit who will walk with her, champion her when she is weak, encourage her when she falters, and stand in the gap when she can't stand. (And the same goes for her partner.) This is the power of agreement.

Remember when the people decided to build the tower of Babel? God came down and discussed the matter with Jesus and the Holy Spirit, that if the people were left to their own devices the power of agreement would enable them to achieve anything they put their hand to. Therefore God scattered them and distributed them to different nations, giving them different languages to diminish their power. This is huge. God knew that if the people continued to speak the same language and agree on the same things, they would become little gods in their imaginations, taking the matters of life and death into their hands and wreaking complete havoc. For the sake of sparing the people from themselves, God created pockets of division (Genesis 11).

Within the realm of marriage, agreement is a powerful tool for the furtherance of God's agenda in the lives of those who have come together. How can two walk together except they be agreed? At the very least, agreed on where they want to go in life. This agreement impacts their progress. If one person is a spendthrift and the other is trying to save, neither one of their objectives is apt to be reached. But if the two agree in order to build their financial pool, both can be satisfied. This principle is one reason God requires couples to submit one to the other. This constant process of dying to self for the greater good of both people creates the synergy needed for the couple to walk in victory. The power of agreement makes them truly a power couple. The enemy knows this, and he is constantly on the prowl to disrupt unity and compromise the effectiveness of the couple's partnership. His modus operandi is always to divide and conquer. Since we know his strategy, we can live offensively and beat him at his own game by not allowing his deceptions to manipulate us.

One way we can do this is by keeping in mind that our interpersonal relationships have a greater purpose than fulfilling our personal desires. Our mates are not here for just our pleasure. They are here also to sharpen us and provoke us to good works. They are here to increase the strength of our character. All fruitful relationships in our lives make us better than we were before our associations with the people we are dealing with. Our husbands should be making us greater women, and we should be making them greater men as we walk together in Christ. As we fulfill the mandate He has placed on our lives and actively walk in His purpose, we will be influencing someone around us for the greater good of God's kingdom.

When others look at our marriages, their standards for how they live their own lives should be raised. Those who don't know Christ should want to know Him based on the witness of our unions. Our relationships should be the salt that gives flavor to our testimonies of the goodness of God so people will thirst to be part of His family—even without us saying anything. What our marriages look like becomes an incredible reflection of God at work in the earth realm… a vision of things to come.

"But what about pleasure?" you ask. Pleasure is the result of our marriages lining up with God's divine design. As we walk in agreement, our partnerships will be fruitful, not just in the area of children but also in the fruit of the Spirit, so that we are productive in the work of our hands and in society. Making significant contributions to our community and inner circles will help us reach out to others, adding to God's kingdom because our lives are good witnesses of Jesus. When we honor our spouses in a way that inspires them to love us like Christ loves the church and gave Himself for it, all of these things culminate and our lives as couples become joyful and vibrant.

Is God interested in our pleasure? Most definitely! It is no accident that He named the garden Eden, meaning "pleasure." It is always His intention that His children experience pleasures evermore by being in His presence, as well as the presence of one another. But abiding in complete harmony with God's will for our lives is a prerequisite to lasting joy. Our Father in heaven knows that a life filled with purpose leads to pleasure.

17

Knowing Your Calling

So the king and Haman came to the feast that Esther had prepared. And as they were drinking wine after the feast, the king said to Esther, "What is your wish? It shall be granted you. And what is your request? Even to the half of my kingdom, it shall be fulfilled" (Esther 5:5-6).

sther surveyed her handiwork and that of her servants. The table was beautifully laid. The finest china and cutlery had not been spared. The king's favorite golden goblets made the table settings as regal as possible.

She watched as the king's eyes lit up with delight at each course presented to him. The food had been prepared to perfection. She was happy that he was happy. The king and Haman chatted away, exchanging pleasantries and robust laughter. She availed herself to make sure they were comfortable and satisfied. She laughed at their jokes, and she even told a few stories of her own. She could see that Haman was quite pleased to be in her presence, relishing this position of favor. He bent over backward to compliment her to the point where she knew he was trying to curry her favor. She remained kind and appeared receptive in spite of the fact that she knew his true deviousness.

Strangely enough, in spite of how well this dinner party was going, she felt no urgency to share why the king and Haman were really here. She was experiencing a peace that passed her understanding. She wondered why she wasn't in a panic to spill the beans before the king. She almost felt sorry that she would be changing the mood of the gathering to something so serious. Her husband was having such a good time. She couldn't recall the last time she'd seen him so relaxed. Again she thought of how rare it was that someone went before him without a request. She wondered if anyone just went before him to pay tribute and render praise without asking for anything in return.

Esther hesitated to interrupt his enjoyment with news sure to cause distress. And now he was asking her again what he could do for her, offering her up to half his kingdom. Such a heady offer! Although it sounded good, she wasn't power hungry. It was, however, flattering to know he thought so highly of her that he was willing to share his power and wealth with her…to make them equal partners of his kingdom.

The king's amazing offer seemed to affect Haman too. But his face betrayed envy and lust instead of awe at the king's generosity. What he truly wanted was what the king was offering Esther. His fight to mask his emotions was obvious.

Esther knew asking for half the kingdom wasn't for her. She didn't believe it was her calling to own kingdoms. No, her mission was to save one. "Who knows if perhaps you were made queen for just such a time as this"—the words of her cousin Mordecai rang in her ears. He was right. Why else would God have permitted such a coupling? She wasn't married to such a powerful king for just her pleasure. No, this was a destiny call.

Esther sat back, her eyes taking in her surroundings. This was no accident or stroke of luck. She was here with a purpose and a specific task in mind. There would be no acquiring of kingdoms today. Besides, all that her husband had she already had access to. He'd made that very clear.

Catching sight of the king's questioning eyes, Esther decided that tonight was not the time to reveal her true intent. It could wait one more day. Tonight was all about the king, about pleasing him. There was a time and season for everything. She felt no prompting from God to broach the subject of the slaughter of the Jews. She trusted the timing to God. Her first calling was to be the king's wife and to be sensitive to his needs. For tonight she would celebrate her husband and make him feel loved.

Marriage can be like a business. The art of negotiation must be practiced at times to get what we need and want from our partners. A woman must understand that even when her husband agrees to share his power, he must still feel powerful. If he feels that his authority is threatened in any way, he will shut down the options or abdicate being his wife's protector and benefactor. To avoid this, we must exercise the art of restraint. "How do we do that?" you ask. There are several things to be sensitive to before pursuing our cause with our mates. Many things can get in the way of getting the results we desire.

First, be sensitive to what is going on in his life. This may take some time and dialog to get a clear read. You'll need to "read the room," as I call it. Is the air around him full of tension? What does his countenance reveal? Is he happy, sad, stressed? You want to remove the distractions in his focus so he can concentrate on you and the issue at hand.

Some problems need to be held in until the right season before they are confronted, depending on the nature of the issue. If your man is under a great deal of stress at work, this is something you know will come to an end. Decide if you can wait for a better time to raise your concern. Remember, your calling as a wife is to take away his stress, not add to it. You want your track record with your husband to be one of speaking the right words in the right season and not taking advantage of when he's down.

The Proverbs 31 wife was an asset to her man by helping him and taking care of her responsibilities. This released him to concentrate on his business and help others, so much so that he became known as a man of integrity and character, highly respected in the marketplace and in the gates of his community. As we look at Proverbs 31 in its entirety we see a well-rounded woman who was into the details of her family to the point that her husband blessed her. He was a satisfied man. Yes, she was a businesswoman and entrepreneur, but it's apparent she also took care of her family and home first. A familiar saying says, "A man wants three things, and then he will be willing to give his woman the world. He wants to be well respected, well loved [in the physical sense], and well fed. When there is no room for complaint, his woman can ask what she wishes, and he will do his best to take care of her."

The wisdom of meeting the other person's needs first is that it cleans the slate of any reason he wouldn't be willing to grant your request. Think of it this way: If you were asking for a raise, you wouldn't want your boss to point to a long list of unfinished tasks or work poorly done to justify his denial of what you asked for, would you? In the same way, your man's willingness to bless you might be contingent on whether he feels loved, honored, and cared for. And before you get rankled, let's be honest. The same holds true for us. We're much more open to hearing a person out and assisting him or her in the dilemma if we're happy and satisfied.

Esther knew her position, and she focused on fulfilling her roles before asking her husband to consider her request. Because of this, he said he was willing to give her up to half his kingdom! This was huge for a king such as him to be willing to surrender any part of what he'd probably fought for. But when a woman's ways please the Lord, she is walking in favor with Him and with her man.

Reflections

❧ When you have a pressing need, what is your approach to your man?

❧ In what ways might you better your approach to him when it comes to sensitive issues?

❧ How do you set the atmosphere and mood so he will be receptive when you share your heart?

Love Talk

God's Word says that discretion will keep you (Proverbs 2:11). So will your intuitive nature. A woman who is keyed into the moods and needs of her man will help her man be the best he can be. And as his heart rests in her because he knows she has his best interest at heart, he will feel free to be the covering God asks him to be.

Be aware of the full extent of your power in your man's life. Never doubt your ability to keep your man's heart and encourage his protection. By understanding and fulfilling your position as his woman on every level, he will move the world to please you.

18

Understanding the Season

*Esther answered, "My wish and my request is: If I have
found favor in the sight of the king, and if it please the king
to grant my wish and fulfill my request, let the king and
Haman come to the feast that I will prepare for them, and
tomorrow I will do as the king has said" (Esther 5:7-8).*

sther weighed the king's offer of up to half his kingdom. Should
she or shouldn't she? He'd given her carte blanche to ask for anything she wanted, but she sensed it wasn't yet time to act. She looked
up and noticed Haman staring at her, as if he was trying to figure out
what she would ask for. She was sure he'd have a million ideas if the
king made the same offer to him. She glanced at her husband. He was
smiling in anticipation of her request. And yet she felt a check in her
spirit. It was a strange situation to be in. One part of her was saying,
"Get while the gettin' is good. You may not get this chance again." But
that was countered by the urgency of the plight of the Jews. She felt in
her spirit that this wasn't the best time to make her request. It seemed
ludicrous to wait any longer with the deadline for the annihilation of
her people looming closer. She had no idea how long it would take the
king to counter his order that approved the murder of her people. Yet

she couldn't press past the leading she felt to wait longer before broaching the subject.

She heard herself calmly inviting the king and Haman to come to dinner the next day. Inwardly she wondered what would be different about tomorrow that could not be accomplished today. The king's pleasure at receiving another invitation to dine with her calmed Esther's thoughts. She realized his happiness would help him be more receptive to her request. She resolved to quiet the storm raging within and exercise patience. She had fasted. She had prayed. She had asked for God's leading. If this was the course of action He was bringing to her, it was best to follow along.

As the king rose, said his goodbyes, and turned to leave, Esther wondered why he hadn't invited her to his chambers or chosen to remain with her. But again she felt led not to press the issue. Perhaps it was best this way, with no distractions from the matter at hand. She needed to remain sharp in spirit to concentrate on hearing God's voice clearly regarding how to move forward.

She wondered if hoping God would handle the subject with her husband was asking too much. She knew her husband didn't place his faith in God. The king had his own way of doing things. Spiritual matters weren't as important to him as they were to her. But God was the God of all. If He could move her husband's heart to select her as queen, He could certainly move him to save His people. All she had to do was wait for His leading.

Though waiting was difficult, she knew God's timing was everything. She'd learned that patience was the tool that often uncovered deception. Everything occurred in its own time and season. To push against God only led to disaster. So, very much against the grain of her own desire, she bid her husband good night. The peace that accompanied her decision confirmed she'd done the right thing. She shook her head. She doubted she'd ever fully understand the ways of God, but she knew she would always choose to trust Him in spite of her own inclinations.

After handling the aftermath of the feast, Esther retired for the night. Gazing into the darkness as she settled into bed, she wondered what the next day would bring.

~~eelllee~~

A wise and prudent woman makes sure her words take effect because she speaks them at the right time. She measures the mood of her man and makes sure that his needs are met before she asks for anything. Esther was a smart woman. She knew when to push and when to hold back. She went about the business of building a great atmosphere for her man to want to do his best for her. She paced herself and attended to her husband's needs first. She trusted God enough not to be in a hurry.

Did you get that? This guiding principle is huge because so much always boils down to it. *Do we trust God enough to let Him handle the timing of emergencies and solutions in our lives?* Do we trust Him to hold down the fort until He's finished organizing our help and deliverance? When we trust Him completely, we won't allow the urgency of our circumstances to rule us or push us into making unwise moves or speaking out of turn.

We need to remember to get out of God's way and let Him deal with the men in our lives. Again, this boils down to trust. If our issue is something God agrees with, He will take our part up for us—if we allow Him to. But the moment we take it into our hands, we are telling God to let go of the reins. The woman who masters the art of silence when everything within is screaming to draw attention to what she wants will find her man being much more open to the leading of the Lord. And this will *always* be to her benefit. God always knows the best timing for everything. I believe the most overlooked fruit of the Spirit listed in Galatians 5 is self-control. Perhaps this is our least favorite because it's the one we struggle most to master. Let's face it, at the end of the day we want what we want and need what we need. We justify our grasping for something because we feel we have a legitimate request. But God's timing is everything no matter how right we believe we are. To be right and act on it at the wrong time can be more destructive than being wrong.

If we speak and act ahead of time, we may think we've attained the desired result, but the victory is never lasting. It's like a plane landing too early at its destination. We still have to wait until we get to the gate to proceed, which can lead to greater frustration. I'll always recall the advice a dear lady offered:

> If you are wrong and the situation is wrong, God says no.
> If you are right but the situation is wrong, God says slow.
> If you are wrong and the situation is right, God says grow.
> And if you are right and the situation is right, God says go.

I've repeated this often because the principle of perfect alignment is so clear. As we remain cognizant of the season and sensitive to the leading of the Lord, we speak at the right time and our words hit their mark. We are speaking in season so they bear the fruit we need at the moment. Only as we cooperate with God's timing do we see the fulfillment of our desires come to pass with lasting effect. When everything is in alignment with God's perfect design, we will always enjoy blessings without any sorrow being added.

Reflections

✗ What is your usual response in those times when you can't see anything going on?

✗ What is your greatest struggle when it comes to waiting on God to act on your behalf?

✗ What stops you from letting go of situations—even when they seem beyond your control?

Love Talk

"There is a time for everything, and a season for every activity under the heavens…a time to tear and a time to mend, a time to be silent and a time to speak" (Ecclesiastes 3:1,7 NIV). Our job is to talk to God and then be still with Him so we will know when the time is right and the Spirit of the Lord is leading us forward. As we lay our issues before Him, He will take up our part if we trust Him and cast our cares on Him because He cares for us (1 Peter 5:7).

19

The Voice of Reason

*So the king and Haman went in to feast with Queen Esther.
And on the second day, as they were drinking wine after the
feast, the king again said to Esther, "What is your wish, Queen
Esther? It shall be granted you. And what is your request?
Even to the half of my kingdom, it shall be fulfilled." Then
Queen Esther answered, "If I have found favor in your sight,
O king, and if it please the king, let my life be granted me for
my wish, and my people for my request" (Esther 7:1-3).*

$\mathscr{E}$sther watched her husband enter the room. His step was even lighter than the day before. She wondered what had occurred to put him in such a wonderful mood. He almost swept her off her feet as he embraced her, so happy was he to see her. What had transpired to so marvelously affect his disposition? Haman, on the other hand, seemed a bit subdued...almost unhappy. He brightened beneath her gaze, but she sensed him struggling to maintain his smile. *Hmm, it is interesting. Interesting indeed,* she thought.

Her curiosity was appeased over dinner as the king shared how he'd been unable to sleep in the middle of the night after leaving her. Perhaps it was the good company and all the wonderful food that had energized him, he said. So he had called for the records of his reign to be read to him, hoping the recitation would help him sleep. But then he heard something that snapped him out of his state of dozing. It was the record of two eunuchs who had transpired to kill him. "Do you remember, Esther? You told me about it." The king went on to say that the records mentioned how Mordecai had gotten word to Esther, and she had relayed it to him. The king paused and gazed at his wife. Yes, his beautiful queen had literally saved his life that day!

Esther lowered her eyes as the passion of his gaze brought heat to her cheeks.

The king went on that since Esther had given credit to her cousin Mordecai, Mordecai should have received his personal thanks. But Mordecai had never been rewarded for his loyalty and faithfulness.

With a flourish the king motioned to Haman. "It was about then that Haman came in." The king shared that Haman had come up with a brilliant suggestion on how to reward someone who pleases the king. He suggested that person be dressed in royal regalia and mounted on the king's own horse. Then one of the king's favorite noblemen should escort the person through the streets and loudly proclaim, "Thus shall it be done to the man whom the king delights to honor" (Esther 6:9). "So I ordered Haman to do exactly that for Mordecai!"

Esther had to focus hard to avoid bursting into peals of laughter. The irony of the situation didn't escape her. No wonder Haman was in such a state. She could imagine how horrified he must have been at having to honor the man he hated so much. The humiliation of his friends seeing him humble himself before the one person they knew he had a vendetta against must have been dreadful. Oh, this was priceless!

She'd wondered why the king hadn't remained after the previous feast after enjoying her company so much. She'd felt within her spirit a prompting to issue another invitation for both men to join her for dinner, which she'd done, so she let it go at that. And now she knew God had been intervening for her even as she slept. She couldn't have done more to curry favor for the Jews than what God had done. In the still of the night, He knew how to appeal to the king and soften his heart. And here was the fruit of God's help. Once again after feasting and thoroughly enjoying regaling Esther with his stories, the king leaned back and said, "What is your wish, Queen Esther?" The look in his eyes said more than his words did as again he offered her whatever she wanted, up to half his kingdom (Esther 7:2).

Esther took a deep breath. This was the moment she'd been waiting for, the time when she knew it was right to present her case to her husband. He was primed to hear her request—his heart prepared by God Himself! Esther searched his face to be sure. *Yes, it was time...*

~eelllee~

Many people overlook the backstory of this time between Esther and her husband. The king had not spent the night with Esther; instead, he'd returned to his quarters. There, in the midnight hour, God kept him awake and orchestrated a surprising occurrence. Through the king's own records, God reminded him of Mordecai and what Mordecai had done to save the king's life. God moved the king's heart to consider how much he owed to Mordecai.

This is such a mighty lesson! Sometimes in our efforts to take command, we speak out of turn. Or should I simply say we talk too much? Some of us are not above beating a dead horse by repeating an issue or situation over and over until we get the response we want. This usually backfires. Our men get tired of listening, and they feel nagged. Their irritation grows over the repetitiveness, and they turn us off or even leave our presence. And if we continue to clamor on, they may shut down and not listen to anyone—including the Holy Spirit. This is where the art of restraint will work for us; if we remain silent, we leave room for the Holy Spirit to work.

Let's consider ourselves mail carriers. Mail carriers simply deliver the mail. They don't follow people into their homes to make sure they open the mail. They don't stand there and force the recipients to read it and follow whatever the mail says. No, they leave it for the receiver to apply at their own discretion. Few times can we really make someone do something. Usually action has to be the person's decision. When people arrive at their own conclusions, they commit more readily to following through on their decisions. But when coerced or manipulated, often they drop the ball.

As has been our theme, we don't need just great timing when it comes to helping people be the best they can be, whether it be boyfriend, husband, boss, or friend. We want to encourage people to want to help us. This means they must have a good disposition toward us. When they want to help us, we can then appeal to them by submitting our needs (as opposed to demanding they be met).

Esther again illustrates this beautifully. She first reminds her husband of how she serves him, not directly but indirectly through her statement that focused on if it was *his* pleasure to assist her. "If I have found favor in your sight, O king, and if it please the king," she said, putting him first (Esther 7:3). Basically she was saying, "If you are pleased with me, and if you want to do something nice for me, here is what I need." Who is going to say no to that? And this is the posture that will help you get the best out of your man. You will be in a submitted place because you're not striving for attention but only for the right results. This is being single-minded in your agenda. It is being selfless and humble. It is a place that few can resist, and so people respond with mercy and grace. This is where a woman can make her man shine.

Reflections

❧ In what ways are you tempted to circumvent waiting for the right moment to take your needs to your mate? What makes you usually feel you should do it immediately?

❧ What has been the result of moving at the wrong time? What have you learned from this?

❧ In what ways do you struggle with pride when broaching important issues with your mate? What do you need to remember to not get distracted by your ego?

Love Talk

Love doesn't demand its own way. It simply loves enough to release the other person to do the right thing. Love empowers people to rise to the occasion of being their best for the other. This is the cycle of giving that occurs in every fruitful relationship.

20

Picking Your Battles

We have been sold, I and my people, to be destroyed, to be killed,
and to be annihilated. If we had been sold merely as slaves,
men and women, I would have been silent, for our affliction
is not to be compared with the loss to the king (Esther 7:4).

Esther saw the look of consternation on her husband's face. She also felt tension emanating from Haman. Still, she kept her gaze locked on the king. She wanted to make sure he understood the import of her words. This wasn't just about her. It was about his kingdom. Here was the angle she needed to help drive her request home. She'd set up a scenario that de-emphasized the fact that she was making an emotional request. She was saying that slavery was something she could live with, but death was a different matter. Haman's decree on the king's behalf would go beyond the king losing his beautiful wife if the mandate was carried out. It would have drastic ramifications on his entire kingdom. The annihilation of all the Jews in his kingdom would seriously affect the workforce, his kingdom's security, and the economy. Haman, in his bitterness, had overlooked the harm he would be doing to the king—the person he claimed such deep allegiance to. Haman's vengeance had been all about him and what he wanted—to the detriment of everyone else. Esther was sure her husband would see this when what she'd said sunk in.

She would make no desperate plea; she would calmly state her case. Again, she put the king first. She knew others bothered him for matters big and small, but she preferred to weigh the issue to see if it was important enough to seek the king's intervention. She never wanted to be a drain or a nag. She wanted to always be a welcome sight, a shelter in the midst of any storm. She never wanted to present a constant clamor or a barrage of requests at every turn. She understood that to win the war, she had to choose her battles wisely, lest she be like the boy who cried wolf and was ignored when the real wolf showed up. She would handle what she could, but allow her husband to step in and be her hero when he could.

Esther watched the king. A slow dawning was coming over his countenance, and soon he was looking at her with such incredulity that she knew her words had hit their mark. With the realization of the consequences, she could see his anger mounting. The king surveyed the room, as if seeking the intruder or madman who would dare perpetrate such a thing. Who could have come up with such a terrible plan? His eyes swept past Haman as the wheels turned in his head.

Esther realized he hadn't quite put two and two together. He didn't know what she was talking about.

Esther said, "I and my people," King Ahasuerus thought.

Esther saw the light coming on in her husband's eyes as the realization that she was Jewish was crystallizing in his mind.

My queen is in danger because of an edict sent out in my name! The king was clearly appalled.

She allowed him more time to process the information she'd given him. She noticed Haman shifting nervously within her peripheral vision, but she refused to look at him. Let him stew in his own juices. For now her focus was her husband and making her request clear. He'd asked her what she wanted—up to half his kingdom. Well, she was pleading for the *entire* kingdom. Not *her* kingdom or even *his* kingdom, of which she was a part. This was no selfish request on her part. She was speaking on behalf of her people.

But she was also speaking for her husband and herself. If she were killed, it would certainly affect him. He had to know this. She completed him. She covered him as much as he covered her. They were one. And Esther had no intention of letting someone like Haman destroy their union or their kingdom. She was very clear on who the enemy was. She just needed to make sure her husband saw him just as plainly.

She knew she had to build her case before she revealed its perpetrator, especially because the king trusted Haman. Esther had to get her husband to sign on to the battle before he might be willing to consider that his friend was the betrayer. Now Haman would be revealed for exactly what he was.

❧

The book of Proverbs mentions the reactions of men to women who nag and carry on clamorous conversations enough times to get us to realize it is an issue we need to pay attention to. It's been said the squeaky wheel gets the grease, but I will venture to say that when the noise is not resolved with grease the next step is to replace the wheel. The danger of constantly complaining and taking issue with every little thing in our relationships is that after a while all the conversations seem to run together. In the midst of the mundane, the urgent gets lost.

We women need to consider a matter carefully before we broach it. Men are such bottom-line people that we can't afford to waste our energy on issues that are of little or no consequence. I call it "using up our favors." Should our men be willing and able to do anything and everything we want? The answer is yes (within reason), but the reality is that they won't. So we must not be slaves to the tyranny of the urgent. Some things are better left unsaid to leave room for conversations that really matter. It's wise to accumulate a bank of good will or points, if you will. The conversation about his socks on the floor or the toilet seat being left up wastes our favors. Let the mundane go. Pick up the socks, put down the toilet seat, and get on with life. These types of habits are not likely to change anytime soon, so we'll only alienate our men and get frustrated ourselves if we decide to be broken records on these types of issues. Majoring on the minors will rob us of the steam we need to discuss more important things, such as finances or a habit they have that harms our relationship. Let's choose the issues we address carefully so when we speak, our words and thoughts are considered important and given priority.

Queen Esther was a master at this. She refused to rush in to the king with insufficient information or with her emotions running high. She didn't nag him about the problem or demand that he do something about it right then. She timed her approach carefully. By the time she made her request, the king was already inclined to be generous toward her. She put him in a position where he could say no, but he'd feel much better about the situation if he said yes. The patience, discipline, and wisdom Esther practiced are earmarks of true prudence. We can practice what we learn from her by considering the cost of our words and deciding if the issue is worth the expenditure of our favors *before* we speak.

Keep in mind that it's not just what we say but how we say it that wins friends and influences people. Just as God resists the proud and gives grace to the humble, men do too. "Inspiring" will always be more effective than "requiring" or "demanding" our way with our men (and everyone else, for that matter). With every need we bring to the table, the issue should be in the interest of both partners. Selfishness is a big turnoff and will always be met with resistance.

We don't want to point out a friend we think is bad for our men if we're doing it based on our feelings alone. Instead, we want to be able to point to the losses and consequences the relationship could incur in his life in a very tangible way so he can see and assess the situation for himself.

At the end of the day, anything we want our men to do has to be something they are moved to do of their own volition. Until the matter is urgent from their viewpoint, we won't get the results we desire. The balance of knowing when to apply gentle pressure but not push too much must be mastered. We want to leave enough time for our men to assess the evidence we give, allow God to intercede on our behalf, come to their own good and godly conclusion, and then act.

Reflections

❧ In what ways have you sabotaged the outcome of your interactions with your mate in the past?

❧ What temptation do you need to resist the most in those instances?

❧ What has been the cycle in those types of situations with your mate? In what ways can you change your approach?

Love Talk

In order to be heard, a person must be willing to hear. In order to be cared for, a person must care. When you sacrifice your rights and empower your man, he will want to meet your expectations as much as possible. This gives you the opportunity to see what he's truly made of. The revelation may surprise you.

Part 6

Where Is the Battle?

hen it comes to relationships, I believe the battle rages on three fronts. It's a subtle fight between the heart, the mind, and the flesh. Though the heart and the mind may be considered, at times, one scripturally and scientifically now that research has substantiated the connection between the two, I separate them for the sake of where we're going simply because we agree that sometimes our intellect doesn't agree with our emotions.

I often say that love isn't brain surgery, but it doesn't hurt to use our heads. And yet, generally speaking, most relationships fall apart because the people involved allow themselves to be ruled by their emotions. Pressed by fear, anger, or pain, words are spoken that can't be retrieved. Drastic actions are taken that can neither be forgotten nor reversed. Accusations and assumptions are made that aren't accurate and drive the "wronged" party to respond in ways that might do further damage.

These are attacks against the power of agreement within a marriage, friendship, business, and wherever fruit can be borne. The enemy understands full well the power of dividing to conquer. What better way to achieve this than through our minds by playing with our thoughts and imaginations? Small wonder we're instructed to bring every imagination under the obedience of Christ (2 Corinthians 10:5). It is only as we retain a submitted thought life that we can have the mind of Christ to see matters clearly. The enemy loves to bring confusion to our minds and relationships to keep us chasing everything but harmony.

Continuously the Bible tells us to go to the party who has hurt or offended us and air our grievances. Why? Because God knows that most of the time the offense has nothing to do with what the offended imagined. And usually it is not the intent of the offender to offend anyone. It is only when we cast down imaginations and get an understanding of the true facts of the matter that reconciliation and harmony can occur. Our minds often can't separate fact from fiction. People say, "It's only a movie," when watching the big screen, but our minds don't process what we're watching as being separate from reality. Small wonder some people copy what they watch on the screen and are shocked when the end turns out differently. In real life people often die when they're shot. In real life relationships suffer drastically from unfaithfulness and offense, sometimes irreparably. This is why the battle for the mind is so significant.

The extreme focus of Esther is a principle that must be embraced and mastered in our relationships because actions and reactions begin in the mind. She stayed honed in on the end result she wanted to achieve and didn't allow herself to be distracted by people or emotions. The mind relays facts that affect our emotions one way or the other, depending on which we allow to take the lead. If we let our emotions rule, we may take a drastic step that will cost us even more in the long run. When we're led by fear, anger, pride, or offense, we will usually take the wrong action. The enemy of our souls loves to wreak havoc on our emotions to make us miss the mark. Nothing can displace the fruit of the Spirit in our lives faster than emotions run amok.

When Samson found out his wife had betrayed him by revealing the answer to a riddle he'd made a wager on, his temper got the better of him. He killed 30 people and paid the debt by giving their clothing to the winners. Then Samson went home, leaving his bride behind. While he was gone, his wife was given to another man by her father. When Samson discovered this, he took vengeance on the Philistines by tying the tails of a hundred foxes together and setting their fields, vineyards, and orchards on fire. This led the wedding guests to take vengeance by killing Samson's wife and her father and burning their house down. So Samson took vengeance by killing many Philistines. And this made the rest of the Philistines take up arms against the Israelites, which resulted in the deaths of more Philistines. So many people affected by one man's emotional outburst! With no thought given to the consequences, Samson allowed his emotions to rule, and it cost him everything.

Even as I write this today, there are news reports of disgruntled employees, people who feel they've been wronged, parents, and others shooting and killing the people around them for vengeance, devastating so many lives.

Haman's Emotional Outburst

Haman had an emotional reaction to Mordecai's refusal to bow before him at the city gates. Instead of reacting against Mordecai alone, he chose to extend his vengeance to the entire Jewish population in the kingdom. Had Mordecai or Esther chosen to respond with the same type and level of emotion, the problem might have continued indefinitely. But they didn't. Instead, they chose to rule over their emotions. They mastered them by submitting the situation to God and awaiting His instructions.

Divine direction is always needed when facing issues caused by and propagated by flawed humanity. Our emotions can drown out the still small voice of God and give rise to dramas no one wants or needs. Esther knew it was imperative that she shut out the voices around her—including her own—and seek God's voice. He alone could help her navigate this situation that threatened her marriage, her life, and the life of her people.

That is the bottom line when it comes to our relationships. The state of our intimate relationships affects every area of our lives. This is why the lines of communication need to stay open and every offense, real or imagined, nipped in the bud. When a marriage is affected, the fallout is never just about the two people directly involved. It affects many others, even ultimately society, as damaged relationships tear the cohesive fabric of families and society. Broken marriages affect children, communities, and even the economy. For this reason, God's first desire is that marriages do not end in divorce. Instead, He entreats us not to let offenses go unaddressed and not to let the sun go down on our wrath (Ephesians 4:26). He encourages us not to give room to the devil so he can gain a foothold and try to make us bitter. God encourages us to walk in love. And if we practice this, we will not be easily offended, quick to rush to judgment, or fast to assume the worst.

Our emotions can cause us to act out in the flesh; therefore, we must master them. The flesh can run rampant when left unchecked. The Bible gives us an overview of the works of the flesh that God would like us to avoid:

> It is obvious what kind of life develops out of trying to get your own way all the time: repetitive, loveless, cheap sex; a stinking accumulation of mental and emotional garbage; frenzied and joyless grabs for happiness; trinket gods; magic-show religion; paranoid loneliness; cutthroat competition; all-consuming-yet-never-satisfied wants; a brutal temper; an impotence to love or be loved; divided homes and divided lives; small-minded and lopsided pursuits; the vicious habit of depersonalizing everyone into a rival; uncontrolled and uncontrollable addictions; ugly parodies of community (Galatians 5:19 MSG).

There you have it. Small wonder we are exhorted to focus on growing in the fruit of the Spirit and putting the works of the flesh to death: "The fruit of the Spirit is love, joy, peace, patience, kindness, goodness, faithfulness, gentleness, self-control" (Galatians 5:22-23). The flesh brings no good into our lives or relationships.

I've told women jokingly for ages that if we want to know what our men are thinking, we should consider what we think and then go the opposite direction. Men and women respond so differently to most situations. And the same is true of God. His ways are not our ways, and His thoughts are not our thoughts. If we are truly daughters of the King, we must remember that He is grooming us not only to be queens but also to behave like them. We are queens of another kingdom, but we are called to be realistic about the battles we fight and the war that is being waged against us as God's children. This war affects our mates, our children, our friends, and us. We must walk alert, recognizing what manner of war we are fighting so we'll know what tools to use and when. There is never a time when the war will be won in the flesh by leaning on our own understanding or the way we feel.

It is critical that we lay down our earthly weapons and utilize heavenly ones. Walking circumspectly and getting still enough to hear our Lord's voice giving us divine direction are the only ways we can reconcile our relationships and heal our hearts when we're hurting. In the end, if we fight with God's help and depend on Him, we will win! Sometimes the victory won't look like what we thought it would, but it will serve the greater good of God's kingdom. And that, my queen, should bless you.

21

Knowing Your Enemy

King Ahasuerus said to Queen Esther, "Who is he, and where
is he, who has dared to do this?" And Esther said, "A foe and
enemy! This wicked Haman!" Then Haman was terrified before
the king and the queen. And the king arose in his wrath from
the wine-drinking and went into the palace garden, but Haman
stayed to beg for his life from Queen Esther, for he saw that
harm was determined against him by the king (Esther 7:5-7).

If Esther hadn't realized the king's anger was not directed at her, she probably would have quaked with fear. In response to her accusation, the king's voice filled the room and boomed, essentially saying, "Who is this person who would dare threaten what is so dear to me?" Esther couldn't have hoped for a better reaction! The king was literally shaking in anger.

Esther could see Haman out of the corner of her eye. He too was shaking—but with fear. His head was moving back and forth and his jaw was slack. Then he was talking inaudibly in his terror. Esther almost laughed at the irony of seeing Haman being moved to pray. Good! He should pray, but his gods surely wouldn't help him. No, he would need to know the one true God to be delivered from his fate.

Standing up, Esther looked at Haman. He seemed to shrink

beneath her gaze. She turned away, looking her husband straight in the face as she pointed to Haman. She didn't look at her enemy as she unflinchingly named him as the perpetrator of the evil she was revealing.

The room exploded with emotional energy. Esther held her breath. She could now hear Haman whimpering behind her. The king's breath was coming in short and harsh bursts. He rose from the place where he'd been sitting. The gold goblet he'd held in his fist slammed into the wall and then clattered to the floor, the loud clamor reverberating around the room. He rose with such force that his chair fell backward with a loud thud. The attendants in the room stood rooted to the spot. No one dared move. Those outside the hall came running at the noise and stopped short when they saw the countenance of the king.

King Ahasuerus suddenly paused and glared at Haman with a look that would have withered any living thing. Then the king turned on his heel and stalked from the room and into the garden as he tried to get a grip on his emotions and decide what to do.

The attendants hesitated before following the king into the garden—keeping their distance just in case he should turn and let his rage spill over on them.

Esther took a deep breath and sank down to her couch. What would her husband do? She'd never seen him this upset. A million thoughts ran through her mind. What was her husband thinking? How would he handle this matter? Though he was her husband and she loved him, she knew of the other side of the king—the one that could enact merciless punishment or pitiless vengeance when he was crossed. She knew approaching the king on behalf of her people had been a dangerous mission from the beginning. She'd risked death to appear before him without being summoned. She'd worried about how to convince him that a colleague he considered a close friend was actually an enemy. This was a sensitive matter that had to be handled just right. And now she ran the danger of the king returning from the garden and refusing to believe that his friend could do something so dastardly. This drama was far from over, and Esther didn't know which way it would turn.

She dared not go after him. The best thing she could do at this point was pray as her husband processed the information he'd been given. She would trust God to help him rise to the occasion, believe the truth, and do the right thing. She prayed his ire wouldn't be redirected to her as the messenger of such ill news. She prayed that God would open the king's eyes to see their enemy and come to her defense. Yes, she had done all she could in following God's instructions. The outcome was up to God.

~☙~

Couples have battled over friends probably since almost the beginning of time. Friendships and relationships can be a very sensitive area. But this isn't the only one. Anytime one partner is right about something and the other one is wrong, the situation can become a hotbed for pride, offense, strife, and a multitude of other fleshly responses. In the midst of misunderstandings and challenges, both partners need to be clear on who the enemy actually is.

Your partner is not the enemy. No, there is a greater foe lurking in the shadows of your life and home. And he has been there from the beginning of time. He did some of his best work in a garden called Eden, and now he is trying to get you to feel you're in an isolated position so he can have a conversation with you like he did with Eve. He wants to convince you to partake of his perverted brand of fruit. If you are unaware that you're not battling against your husband or even against flesh and blood, you will be in trouble, and your attempts to find a healthy solution and outcome will be to no avail. Your battle is against principalities and spiritual wickedness in high places. These unseen forces do their best work in the invisible realm that manifests in our lives here on earth.

The other thing you need to know so that you can stay focused is the enemy is not really interested in you. His agenda is far more sinister. He is aiming at the heart of God. Oh yes, his vendetta is against God for ousting him out of his favored position and casting him down from heaven. How better to get back at God than to hurt what matters to Him most? That's right—you and me.

Relationships, especially marriage because it foreshadows on earth what will take place in heaven, is a reflection of what being one with God looks like. Satan wants to mar that picture. Unfortunately for him, he always overplays his hand and it backfires. Just like Haman did, and his vengeance certainly backfired on him. Haman didn't really care about the Jews. He was mad at Mordecai. The best revenge against Mordecai was to strike at the heart of those he cared about most— God's people, the Jews. But like Satan, Haman didn't have all the facts. He didn't know the queen was Jewish and related to Mordecai.

When conflict arises, if a couple would stop seeing each other as the one at fault and realize who the real enemy was in their midst, they would probably tackle their issues differently. Gone would be the accusations and arguments because there would be no need to defend oneself. Walls of pride wouldn't go up. Real conversations and transparent vulnerability would move them to cover one another in a new way.

Trials would bring them closer instead of widening the gap between them. They would join together in times when tension says to separate. And before a negative word could be spoken, they would pray for unity and wisdom. They would rely on the intervention and counsel of God to see them through hard times.

Unfortunately, this isn't something we tend to do. We must see the wisdom of this approach on our own. We can't be told to handle situations this way because we'd naturally rebel. No, we must come to the spiritual understanding of the fact that a spiritual enemy lurks in the shadows and then trust God to guide us.

When you decide not to look at your husband as the enemy, you will no longer be a vessel the enemy can easily use to create disharmony in your relationship. When the enemy is exposed, his power dissipates. You will approach your husband from a different place in your heart, and your loving, compassionate attitude will win him to your side. Your changed posture will speak for you and help you achieve greater things than an accusatory or defensive stance can. He will move from defending himself to defending your interests, and you will do the same for him.

Reflections

❧ Who is usually blamed when challenges arise in your relationship? Why?

❧ When you take a step back from a difficult situation, are you usually able to see the enemy's strategy at work?

❧ When you recognize Satan's tactics, what can you do to help your husband see them as well?

Love Talk

The woman who is able to recognize and expose the enemy lurking behind her husband's back will gladden the heart of her man. The enemy loves to strike at the heart of trust between a man and a woman. When a woman covers her husband, he rests in the fact that he can trust her. He will not fear being exposed in any situation because his woman has shown she is on his side and will champion him. And when you know your man has your back and will champion you, you feel confident and secure. This makes your partner and you a solid team—a strong, three-strand cord with Christ at the center of your relationship.

22

The Heart of a True Man

*The king returned from the palace garden to the place where
they were drinking wine, as Haman was falling on the couch
where Esther was. And the king said, "Will he even assault the
queen in my presence, in my own house?" As the word left the
mouth of the king, they covered Haman's face. Then Harbona,
one of the eunuchs in attendance on the king, said, "Moreover,
the gallows that Haman has prepared for Mordecai, whose
word saved the king, is standing at Haman's house, fifty
cubits high." And the king said, "Hang him on that." So
they hanged Haman on the gallows that he had prepared for
Mordecai. Then the wrath of the king abated (Esther 7:8-10).*

Esther struggled to sit aright. It had happened so quickly the servants hadn't even had time to react. Haman had thrown himself
on top of her. This was the first pang of fear she'd felt. She wasn't sure
of his intention. Haman was heavy as he leaned against her, grasping
at whatever he could like a man drowning. He was pleading for his
life as beads of sweat covered his forehead and his breath came out in
gasps. Esther looked into his fear-filled eyes and didn't know what to
say. He was feeling the same fear her people would feel if the mandate
against their lives was enforced. She steeled her resolve not to pity him.

As she tried to extricate herself from beneath him, her husband reentered the room. He stopped short just for a second at the sight of Haman in a questionable position pressed against his wife. The room crackled with electricity as the king bellowed and rushed toward the fiend. The king's words rang through the air like an alarm. "Would you assault the queen in my presence!"

Haman struggled to rise and explain, but words weren't coming easily. He gasped for air, strangled by his fear of what was surely to come. He frantically motioned a negative in response to the king's accusation. No, he was not trying to violate the queen. This was a misunderstanding. He wilted to the floor exhausted by his own efforts to regain his composure just as the servants rushed to take hold of him.

It wasn't a moment too soon. The king glared at him with the utmost contempt even as the attendants threw a cloth over Haman's face. Then, remembering Esther, the king's gaze shifted to her. Concern and softness washed away his anger. "Are you okay?" he asked gently.

Before Esther could answer, the moment of tenderness was cut short by Harbona, one of the king's eunuchs. He looked equally upset as he took in the situation. He then informed the king that Haman had constructed gallows to hang Mordecai on.

There it was—the last bit of evidence that Esther had been correct, that her accusation again Haman wasn't a personal vendetta. This was a very real wake-up call for the king regarding his former friend's character. Now that it had been clarified, there was no way the king was going to allow this man—this Haman who had blatantly disrespected the queen—to live. It took only a moment for him to respond. So Haman had built gallows to hang Mordecai? Haman wanted to kill the same Mordecai he'd been ordered to lead through town and honor in the presence of everyone for his service to the king? Fair enough. The king lifted his hand and pointed at Haman. "Hang him on that."

The king watched the eunuchs carry Haman away, the prisoner whimpering like a dog. Now that Haman was gone, a wave of exhaustion swept over the king. He walked to Esther and held her close. She was safe.

This is where the men get separated from the boys. A true man will defend his woman, protecting her at all costs. One of his missions is to be her hero. I have such a passion for Esther in particular because she was married to a heathen king. He didn't believe in the God of the Israelites, and King Ahasuerus probably had no appreciation of her culture or her spiritual beliefs. He had his own gods and his own ways of viewing the world. Many women are in this situation today. They are married to unbelievers or men who aren't as passionate about God as they are. This affects their marriage relationships, especially when things come up that are of importance, because they are looking at the issues from two very different perspectives. Esther didn't dwell on the king's lack of spirituality or the fact that he wasn't a believer in her God. She trusted that God was greater than her husband's heart and beliefs and able to move on her behalf. Esther was able to bridge the gap by finding common ground. They both cared about one another. As she cared for his interests, he rose to the occasion and cared for hers.

I'd like to make a very critical observation: *Esther allowed her husband to be her hero.* She didn't try to take care of Haman herself. She didn't interrupt or interfere with the king as he dealt with the situation. She submitted her situation to her man and left room for him to act as he saw fit. She allowed him to feel like a knight in shining armor.

After teaching one day, I was asked why life was so difficult for so many women. I was a bit surprised by the question. I've always enjoyed being a woman, and I've never viewed it as a hardship. I answered that God hadn't designed life to be so trying for women, but women often complicate their lives when they try to be men. Anytime people operate outside of God's design, they step outside His grace. That makes life hard and laborious. Though many women are masters of self-sufficiency, a woman often struggles with how to turn over the reins when a special man comes into her life. Yet all the while they complain of exhaustion and how they wish they had someone to share their lives with. If this is really true, when a man enters your life you must make him feel significant and allow him to be who he was created to be in your life. The woman who "wears the pants" in the relationship runs the risk of becoming resentful of the man she so deeply wants.

Resentment leads to disrespect. Once that sets in, lack of desire follows, which often leads to the demise of the relationship. At the end of the day, every woman wants a man…but he will not be a man unless a woman allows him to be one.

In a world where songs such as "Sisters Are Doin' It for Themselves" are popular, many women have grown weary of doing so. The tension between men and women has grown to an all-time high as the cycle of disappointment is perpetuated. Men resent women who won't allow them to be whom they were created to be. And women resent men who will not rise to the occasion to treat them as God intended. "Where are the true men?" they ask. The answer is that they are still here, but most of them have abdicated their roles and responsibilities. Many men will not fight for their position with their women; instead, they will simply step aside and let their women do their own things.

I've had conversations with many women who mentioned activities they were doing that their husbands should be doing. When I asked why, they all said the same thing: "Oh, he doesn't mind" or "He doesn't have a problem with it." I simply raise my eyebrows. Later I usually hear a completely different story from the husband. In frustration he raises his hands as he says he's tried to speak with his wife on the subject, but she doesn't listen. He's grown so weary that he now refuses to fight about it.

Not only has he abdicated on this area with his wife, but his emotions have also been affected. In a man's world, defeat affects his desire for his wife. Every man longs to be his wife's hero and her king. If he isn't allowed to be king at home, he will find another kingdom to rule. Whether it be work, a hobby, another woman—he will find something or someone who makes him feel on top of his game.

Recently I was watching a film where the man was plotting to leave his wife. It was finally revealed that he was leaving her for a woman he felt needed him. His wife had become successful and self-sufficient. She even knew how to fix her own car. She had no need for him. I once heard a pastor say, "If both of you are alike, then one of you is unnecessary." Distrust and pride play a great part in dismantling the ability of your man to become your hero.

Pride tells a woman she doesn't need a man. The truth of the matter is that women do need men and men need us. God created us to be relational and interdependent, so this is a natural, God-given need. Second, we must not play into the hands of the enemy and listen to his lies that suggest that "all men are dogs," "all men are unfaithful," or "all men are weak." These generalizations will never be true because no woman will have the opportunity to experience all men. For every quip like this about men, there are similar statements men make about women.

If we will get back to the basics of what we want and need in partners, we will release them to be what they were created to be. God says to cast all our cares on Him because He cares for us (1 Peter 5:7). God wants to be God in our lives. He wants us to bring our cares to Him so He can address them, solve them, and reveal His power. A man desires the same thing. The maddening thing about God and the men in our lives is they seldom move according to our timetable. And the fear that they will not follow through sometimes causes us to want to take the matter into our own hands. Resist this urge! As we trust that God's timing is perfect, we can also trust God to work through our mates to provide what we need at just the right time. The proof is in the story. As we allow God to be God, and as we allow our men to answer the call to be the men God wants them to be to us, we will find that we are no longer damsels in distress. We will find we already have the heroes we've been looking for.

Reflections

✻ In what areas have you taken charge of your life? How influenced are you by the "tyranny of the urgent"?

✻ What has been your mate's typical response in the past when you don't wait for him to act?

✻ In what areas do you feel your partner has abdicated his responsibility? In what ways might your conversations, attitudes, and actions contribute to this?

Love Talk

Every little girl dreams of being rescued by a dashing prince on a white horse. I believe this desire is spiritual and not just conditioning from reading too many fairy tales. After all, Jesus Christ, the ultimate bridegroom, will return on a white horse to carry His bride, the church, away. He has rescued us from our afflictions—namely sin. Because so much is parallel between the spiritual realm and the natural, it's no wonder that women look for heroes in their men. This is a God-given expectation that will only be realized if we allow our men to be the heroes they were created to be. In the postures of Snow White waiting to be awakened from her poison-induced sleep and Rapunzel letting her hair down from a lofty tower, we too must be willing to awake and release ourselves into the arms of those who long to rescue us. Then and only then will we be able to breathe, "My hero!"

23

Reaping What We Sow

On that day King Ahasuerus gave to Queen Esther the
house of Haman, the enemy of the Jews. And Mordecai
came before the king, for Esther had told what he was to
her. And the king took off his signet ring, which he had
taken from Haman, and gave it to Mordecai. And Esther
set Mordecai over the house of Haman (Esther 8:1-2).

What a whirlwind! So much had occurred it was still taking Esther time to process everything. She'd gone from wondering if the king would honor her request to save her people to being given the house, property, and assets of the man who wanted to kill all the Jews. It was hard to believe Haman was really gone.

Haman hadn't really had time to figure out what hit him. He went from celebrating being invited to dine with the king and the queen to being dragged unceremoniously from Esther's apartments to the gallows. That was quite different than the picture of the future he'd had in mind. He'd congratulated himself on being able to come up with such a great scheme to wreak revenge on his enemy, Mordecai. Instead, it was just like his friends had warned: "If Mordecai...is of the Jewish people, you will not overcome him but will surely fall before him" (Esther 6:13).

I believe what they were saying is that if the God of the Jews was truly the God they'd heard about, Haman didn't stand a chance going against Him. So Haman should desist from any attempt to ruin them. But he hadn't listened, so confident was he about his "in" with the king. And then it seemed he even had a connection with the queen. Imagine his horror upon discovering the people he had a vendetta against included the queen. I'm sure he thought he was in a horrible nightmare. But no, it was reality. He was dragged to the very gallows he'd had built for Mordecai and put to death.

Esther shook her head again at the recollection. The king had given the keys to Haman's house to her and declared all his property hers. She had no need for it, and certainly no desire to step foot in it. She felt it was only right to give it to her cousin Mordecai. Yes, it was time he was rewarded for his due diligence to her and to the king. She knew it was time to reveal the rest of her story to her husband. She was tired of keeping secrets. King Ahasuerus had proven he could be trusted with who she was; therefore, she would share with him completely. The light of understanding came into his eyes as she revealed her connection to Mordecai.

The king summoned Mordecai immediately. When he arrived, the king thanked him for all he'd done. Then to Esther's delight, her husband presented Mordecai with his signet ring. The very same ring he'd given to Haman! This ring gave Mordecai the authority to act on the king's behalf.

Mordecai was at a loss for words.

Esther touched her cousin's hand. No words were needed. She beamed with pride. She was impressed and heartened by Mordecai's commitment to God and to their people. He'd stood unwavering while some Jews had compromised their standards to fit in with the society they'd found themselves in. Mordecai refused to bend his knee or any part of his life to anyone or anything but the one and only true God. And now it had paid off richly. If there was ever proof that God was faithful to those who were faithful to Him, this was it. Vengeance truly belonged to God, and He had taken care of Haman.

◦ⅇⅇⅉⅉ◦

When it comes to caring for and protecting His people, no one does it better than God. The knowledge of this has delivered me from the desire to walk in unforgiveness or correct those who have wronged me. As we release our enemies into God's hands, they will reap what they sow and fall into their own traps.

Generally speaking, we associate reaping and sowing more in the negative. But it's also important to look at the principle of sowing and reaping in the positive sense of how they work in our relationship with God, our mates, and others. Consider sowing like having a bank account. The more we deposit into the love bank with our mates, the more the interest accrues between us. The more we have in our love bank account, the easier it is to make withdrawals when needed. However, if we keep making withdrawals with no deposits, we will soon find ourselves bankrupt.

The same goes for our relationship with God. Mordecai was a praying man who remained faithful to God no matter what. He was not moved by peer pressure or even legal authority to compromise God's standards. He stayed true to God, and when he found himself in a place of dire need, God more than delivered. He came through for Mordecai in a way that exceeded his expectations. Not only did He save Mordecai from danger, but He also dispensed of his enemy and delivered the enemy's worldly goods to him (through Esther) as a reward for his faithfulness. God rewarded Mordecai for his faithfulness amid all the trauma and drama. Mordecai sowed richly into his relationship with God and reaped a rich return.

Esther sowed not only into her relationship with God but also into her relationship with her husband. She sowed the seeds of faithfulness, loyalty, love, and honor. She took care of her husband, feeding him and catering to his needs. She sowed great seeds of satisfaction and fulfillment into her man. These were seeds that took root and grew, producing a fine harvest of fruit that sustained them both. They were partners who had each other's backs. His heart rested in his wife and he trusted her. In a palace filled with intrigue and hundreds of selfish agendas, she had remained true to serving him. She made healthy deposits into her love bank. And she reaped the rewards by having a husband who loved her and protected her. She'd won his heart and his allegiance to protect her and provide for her. Her deposit was so rich into his life that he offered her riches in exchange—up to half his kingdom. This is a great example of the law of sowing and reaping.

Are you aware that the heart of a man is competitive? Like God, he will try to not allow you to out-give him. The more you give to him, the more he will want to give to you. When I say this, I'm not addressing the material world. I'm talking about the intangibles of life, about sharing your kindness, your smile, your loving countenance, your listening ear, your love, trust, understanding, and encouragement. These pay huge dividends in a man's world. He longs for them; he must have them. And if he doesn't get them from you, he will look for them elsewhere.

Sowing into Your Man's Life

We women need to determine what we want to receive from our men and then make sure we sow that into our relationships. Do you want your man to have a listening ear? Then you need to listen to him. Some of the things you desire may not be things he is comfortable with or has been exposed to. If that's the case, it's up to you to model those things and liberate him to follow suit. For instance, some men didn't see affection modeled during their growing-up years, so they need to be taught how to be affectionate. Show your man what your brand of affection looks like. Learn to speak his language. Find out what is important to him. Listen to the things he talks about, the things that get him excited. Tap into the things he reveals and support them. As you sow into his life in the areas that are important to him, he will want to follow suit in yours.

Help your partner know what you want. Tell him in a loving way, and show him through your actions. Men do not have ESP. Being clear about what you want and need from your man by speaking the truth in love helps him to be confident in providing for you. It helps him avoid the frustration of not being able to figure out what you want and need. Help him to help you. He will be a willing pupil when he knows he can trust you and that you want him to be your man. Let him know your needs. Sow what you want to reap.

Reflections

✗ How have you expressed what you want or need from your mate in the past?

✗ In what ways do you model for him the things you would like from him?

✗ How do you reinforce and encourage your man when he does something you like?

Love Talk

The Word of God tells us it is better to give than to receive, but there is more. If you give, you will receive what you give and more. This is the law of sowing and reaping. One seed produces more fruit than what you planted. As you sow into the life of your husband and loved ones, the returns will be greater. God takes note of your giving and adds to it. The harvest always stretches past the amount sowed. So give with an open heart, not seeking a return but simply experiencing the joy of depositing seeds that will bear fruit—and not just in the kingdom of God but in your own kingdom as well.

24

The Power of Vulnerability

*Then Esther spoke again to the king. She fell at his feet and wept
and pleaded with him to avert the evil plan of Haman the
Agagite and the plot that he had devised against the Jews. When
the king held out the golden scepter to Esther, Esther rose and
stood before the king. And she said, "If it please the king, and
if I have found favor in his sight, and if the thing seems right
before the king, and I am pleasing in his eyes, let an order be
written to revoke the letters devised by Haman the Agagite,
the son of Hammedatha, which he wrote to destroy the Jews
who are in all the provinces of the king. For how can I bear
to see the calamity that is coming to my people? Or how can I
bear to see the destruction of my kindred?" (Esther 8:3-6).*

Esther knew her work wasn't yet done. It was one thing to have her
husband deal with Haman, but that enemy was merely the one
who had planted the seeds of destruction. Even now the weeds were
spreading throughout the communities of the kingdom. She knew
she had to get the king to reverse the order before the fateful day came
when genocide would break out throughout their domain and the Jews
would be slaughtered. She didn't want to appear ungrateful for all her
husband had done for her and given to her, but the situation was still
far from concluded.

How could she sleep at night knowing her people were still in danger? She could not! Owning Haman's house and seeing him hanged didn't abate the urgency she felt to procure the safety of the Jews. She didn't want to overload the king with endless requests, yet this one she couldn't contain.

She would appeal to the king—that if she'd given him any pleasure and if he thought it was the right thing to do, to please reverse the decree Haman had made in the king's name. Esther would depend on the king's understanding and experience to come to her aid. She prayed that he would be in agreement with her. Daring to come into his presence again uninvited, she tried to contain her emotions.

She stood at the door of the throne room waiting for him to notice her, waiting to see if he'd be willing to see her again. Suddenly she became aware of the silence around her. Looking up, she saw that the king was smiling and extending his scepter to her once more. He beckoned her forward. Esther could no longer pretend to be strong and stalwart. She was in desperate need of his intervention, and she needed him to know the extent of it. Weeping, she moved forward. Tenderly she touched the tip of his scepter and then looked into her husband's eyes. She did not avert her gaze. She needed him to be mindful of her plea more than ever before. She simply couldn't stay safely behind the palace walls while her people were slaughtered.

She appealed to him with everything that was in her. She hoped she would make a good case for her request. Though the king extended the scepter and gave her permission to come forward, she was well aware the power to make a difference really belonged to him. In his kingdom, he alone could avert this tragedy. She couldn't circumvent his authority. Yes, she was his queen, but he was the king. She was a wife submitted to her husband. Though she could make her wishes known, having them fulfilled would only happen if her husband said they would.

Esther needed the king to call a halt to Haman's madness. The time of mass murder was drawing nigh. Perhaps it was the urgency of the matter that reduced her to tears, but she was not ashamed. Now was not the time for pride. She needed his intervention. In that moment she forgot about herself completely and focused on safety for her people. The king had proved faithful before, and she prayed he would again. She hoped he would hear her heart and know that granting this request would mean more to her than any material possession ever could. Searching his face, she dared not try to read his mind. She took a deep breath and made her request. The she held her breath and waited for his response.

〰️

The world has done a number on women in general. So often we feel there is no place for femininity and gentleness in the marketplace and even in our personal relationships. "Never let them see you sweat or cry" seems to be the mantra. "Vulnerability" has become a bad word today. No damsel dare be in distress before her prince anymore. Oh no! She must be strong and unflinching. But then the Scripture comes to my mind that simply states, "God opposes the proud, but gives grace to the humble" (James 4:6). Well, so do people. Pride throws up walls and signals we don't need help.

There is a lot of powerful persuasion in a woman's tears. Most men can't bear to see women cry. Tears are like a fire they are frantic to put out. Many years ago I was driving in Los Angeles and made a wrong turn. Before I'd even completed the turn, a policeman was flagging me down. For a moment I was distracted by the fact that he was really cute...until he asked me for my driver's license. To my horror, I realized I didn't have it with me. I'd switched purses that morning and left it in my other bag. I was mortified, and I knew I was in deep trouble. This was one of many things that had gone wrong that morning. I couldn't take it anymore, and I crumpled under the weight of all the trauma, including the impending legal trouble. I burst into tears right there on the spot as I wailed that I couldn't find my driver's license.

The poor officer became totally flustered. He made suggestions for where I could look to find my license. He was so sorry that I was in such a state that he sought to calm me down. He suggested I didn't have to worry. All I would have to do was go to traffic school for a day in lieu of paying the violation and having it put on my driving record. I tearfully thanked him and continued on my way. My tearful apology for violating the law let him know I was sincerely repentant and not blatantly disregarding the law. It softened his heart toward me, and in this case lightened the consequence of my misdeed.

Now, I'm not suggesting that we deliberately cry to manipulate men (or anyone). What I am saying is that when we remain authentic and vulnerable, we open the door for the hearts of our men to feel our pain and the depth of our need so they will choose to respond in a way that alleviates our distress. Remember, our men want to be our heroes. What more wonderful task can they do than rescue us from trouble and despair?

Yes, perhaps our needs aren't as deep or urgent as people being annihilated, but our needs are very real to us no matter what scale they are on. So be real. Approach your man from a tender place where he is free to address your needs with confidence and sensitivity. Be transparent in your feelings. When you hurt, let him know it by inviting him into your heart, into the sanctuary where the real you resides. In Song of Solomon, the king said of his bride, "You are my private garden, my treasure, my bride" (4:12 NLT). Only he has the key. The king proclaimed this proudly. His woman was truly his, and only he was invited to know her intimately. The connotation in Song of Solomon is of physical intimacy, but it also is implied for the inner sanctum of her heart.

Nothing binds two people together more than praying together, secrets shared, and overcoming adversity in unity. I'm talking the deep things about ourselves that we don't share with anyone except the ones we love. Our partners know when they don't have access to all of us. Until those moments when they feel they have gained all of our heart and all our trust, they will not feel like they possess us fully. And men are possessive by nature. They will protect what belongs to them...but they must know we really belong to them and they have permission to act. They want access to the parts of us that no one else gets to see or experience. We must be their treasure.

Though letting your guard down may seem scary if you've been hurt, it's an even scarier notion to never be rescued from your ivory tower simply because you refused to let your hair down. Remember, you are not making yourself vulnerable to just anyone. This is your man. You are submitting to your husband, not just spiritually but also emotionally. This is the man you trust, that you have chosen to bond with. This is the man who is your harbor in any storm. Rest in his love, and let him care for you. Let him see you as you are. Trust God to work in him, trust the power of God to turn your husband's heart toward you and your concerns. Rest in the knowledge that God is able to fill the gaps your man can't.

It takes more energy to keep your guard up than to drop it and allow yourself to be helped. So take a deep breath, turn to your man, and let it all out.

Reflections

✕ What keeps you from being completely transparent with your man? What has negatively affected your trust in him in the past?

✕ What has positively affected your trust in him?

✕ What fears do you harbor about being vulnerable?

✕ What part does God play in your interactions with your partner?

Love Talk

Every woman dreams of a man who will rescue her from the fearsome dragon and take her away to the land of Happily Ever After. But that ending is guaranteed by Christ alone. In the meantime, God offers you a foretaste of heaven here on earth if you are willing to die daily to yourself and your fears, daring to be vulnerable with your husband because you know that ultimately the Lord covers your heart and hears your soul cry. As you trust Him to interpret your deep longings to your partner, you will be blessed by his response to your need. And that's extremely romantic.

Part 7

What Is True Victory?

$\mathcal{I}$n a world where everyone is jockeying for position, we can lose sight of the purpose of relationships. A war should never be between two people in a loving relationship. Neither is there any place for competition. In a committed relationship, teamwork should be at an all-time high. The enemy in his tirade against mankind loves to cause confusion and chaos by creating contests between partners. In the midst of the confusion, we tend to adopt a false sense of what "victory" is.

Many people have made their point and proven they were right, but they found themselves standing alone after the dust settled. This question needs to be asked at strategic times: Do I want to be right or do I want to have a solid, loving relationship? When you answer yes to the loving relationship, this is where dying to self comes in. God's Word tells us that those who seek to save their lives will lose it, and those who seek to lose their lives for Jesus's sake will find life (Matthew 10:39). Just as Christ laid down His life and received all things for us, we are called to lay down our rights and our lives for Him on a daily basis. This is righteousness for His name's sake. We do the right things in our relationships because it glorifies God and makes Him look good. But we also do them to make things work for the good in our relationships.

The highest form of human relationship calls us to die to self to become one with our partners. This is not a one-time destination that we reach and that's it. No, becoming one is a *process of unfolding*, of different layers of who we are, our experiences, and our mindsets coming off. Think of an onion. The more layers we peel back, the stronger the essence of the onion is experienced. I'm sure you know what I mean. The insides are exposed, and the air is filled with the pungent aroma. Yet it is this onion and its accompanying odor that adds flavor to food to make it more delicious.

Becoming one as a couple is a journey, and it takes both people in the car to get to the destination. If a couple keeps fighting along the way, they will eventually crash. If the goal is getting to a place called One, contests, rivalry, and being at odds need to be done away with through communication and love. We need to not focus on making our points or showing the other what we know.

What is "victory"? It's two people becoming truly one. And they become one when each person chooses the better good for the sake of both of them so both people can be fruitful and prosper. It's not about one person getting his or her way. In a committed relationship, it's *always* about both people.

A profound principle is found in a statement Jesus made: "For this reason the Father loves me, because I lay down my life that I may take it up again. No one takes it from me, but I lay it down of my own accord. I have authority to lay it down, and I have authority to take it up again" (John 10:17-18). That is deep. To those who don't understand the nature and power of Christ, the Romans killed Jesus and He was helpless to do anything about it. And yet nothing is further from the truth! When He was being arrested and Peter drew his sword to help, Jesus said to him, "Do you think that I cannot appeal to my Father, and he will at once send me more than twelve legions of angels? But how then should the Scriptures be fulfilled, that it must be so?" (Matthew 26:53). And yet when questioned on His identity as the Son of

God, Jesus merely answered, "You say that I am" (Luke 22:70). He who had the greatest point to prove chose to not prove any point at all. He focused on His great love for us and was willing to be despised, humiliated, and put to death to win us to Himself. The utmost of meekness and humility is to display these strengths in our relationships with one another.

What point do you have to prove? At the end of the day is it really worth it if proving you're right alienates the very person you so badly want to impress? I've heard people say, "I'll show them I'm nobody's fool." My reaction? "Well, if you know it, why bother trying to prove it?" It's been said, "Never explain yourself to anyone because the person who loves you doesn't need it and the person who doesn't love you won't believe you anyway." But the greater point is, "If you have to do too much show and tell, perhaps you are protesting too much for a reason." The substance isn't there to support the point you're trying to make.

When trying to encourage a specific outcome within a relationship, we must have our priorities in line. What is most important to us? Do we want to make a point to promote the good of our relationships or simply to best our partners? What is the motive behind our conversations and our actions?

All of this boils down to "rights" within a relationship. Rights are why we get angry if we don't feel our partners are heeding our point of view. We feel violated. After all, we have the right to be heard and responded to in a certain way—at least that's what we think. Esther approached the king with the attitude that she had no rights, and she got everything she wanted. She was willing to strip herself of title, position, and circumstance to get what she requested from the king. Consider Jesus. He was so consumed with the desire to redeem us and claim us for His own that He didn't consider the requirement to leave heaven and come to earth to die in our place too much to pay. The bottom line in this discussion is how badly do we want what we want or need? What are we willing to do to get it? Is it really important for us to get credit? Or is it more important that our request be met and fulfilled?

We need to embrace the fact that we really have no rights in Christ.

Our rights are hidden in our Lord and Savior, who sacrificed everything and laid His life on the line for us. He stood as a lamb before His shearers in silence, offering no protests and no defense to gain everything for us. He is seated at the right hand of the Father, calmly waiting for the fulfillment of God's plan as outlined in Scripture. Nowhere is it recorded that Jesus stuck out His tongue at the devil. Yes, Jesus bested Satan, but He didn't brag about it because that wasn't the main point of Jesus's coming. He knew in advance He would defeat the devil (Matthew 16:18; Hebrews 2:14; 1 John 3:8). The primary focus of Jesus was restoring the relationship between people and God. He came to rescue His bride—the church (people who trusted Him as their Savior and Lord)—from a condition she could not escape from on her own.

That's what partners do for each other! Christ could have found fault with us. He could have rightfully accused us of being unresponsive, stubborn, hard-hearted, unappreciative of His efforts to reach out to us. He could have used a hundred excuses to give up on us. He could have shown us who was wrong and who was right, who was holy and who was not. Instead, He chose to not engage in arguments but to come to earth and die for us so we could be with Him forever.

Jesus didn't want to coerce us or force us into following Him. No one likes to have people cave in to his or her wishes because they felt badgered, belittled, or manipulated. The Word tells us God likes a cheerful giver. So do we! We want to be heard and understood, and we want our wishes to be addressed and fulfilled with enthusiasm and care. This is what makes us feel loved and significant. When it comes to our partners, family, friends, and coworkers, we want to know that they want for us what we want for ourselves. Why? Because that shows that their hearts beat in harmony with ours. When it comes to our mates, as we grow together in the process of becoming one, we are walking in agreement on more and more things. We begin to love what our partners love. We develop like minds.

Have you noticed how couples who have been together for a long time begin to look alike? Some even finish each other's sentences. This is oneness! Over the years I've asked couples who have been together for a long time about their secret to staying together. Most have said the same thing: Pick your battles carefully and always choose to forgive. These couples champion each other. They've learned that relationships are not contests or an arena for a battle of wills. They've found that victory is when they both win by choosing those things that work to the greater good of them both.

25

The Secret of Authority

Then Esther spoke again to the king. She fell at his feet and wept and pleaded with him to avert the evil plan of Haman the Agagite and the plot that he had devised against the Jews... Then King Ahasuerus said to Queen Esther and to Mordecai the Jew, "Behold, I have given Esther the house of Haman, and they have hanged him on the gallows, because he intended to lay hands on the Jews. But you may write as you please with regard to the Jews, in the name of the king, and seal it with the king's ring, for an edict written in the name of the king and sealed with the king's ring cannot be revoked" (Esther 8:3,7-8).

$\mathcal{E}$sther hoped she wasn't overstepping her boundaries by asking for yet another thing. After all the king had been generous enough to do away with Haman and give her his house. She didn't want to beat a dead horse, but the seeds Haman had planted needed to be destroyed completely lest they sprout again. And there was the matter that Haman had so smoothly gotten the king to agree to and sign an edict authorizing the murder of the Jews. Everyone knew that once the king decreed something, it was established and couldn't be revoked. How could the work Haman set in motion be stopped?

Mordecai stood resolutely by Esther's side as she pleaded with the king. Then they stood before Ahasuerus awaiting his verdict. The king looked at them and pondered his next move. He knew he couldn't revoke the order that had already been sent. No one was allowed to change what went out under his name and with his seal. However, another order could be written that would, in essence, be superimposed on what he'd already written. Yes, that was the solution!

He wasn't familiar enough with the mindset of the Jews or what would be fair terms to them, so he released that responsibility to Mordecai, who had proven himself to be wise and trustworthy. With that, the king summoned his scribes. He informed them they would take dictation from Mordecai. Whatever he commanded them to write should be written.

Turning to Mordecai, King Ahasuerus instructed him to write what he thought was best and he would stand behind it. He'd given him his signet ring, and Mordecai should seal the order with it so the edict would be carried out just as he had written.

Mordecai bowed deep and low to the king, thanking him for his generosity. Then he drew himself up to his full stature and faced the scribes who awaited his words. He ordered that all the Jews in the kingdom could stand their ground and fight if any citizen of the kingdom came against them. No one who was hostile toward them should be spared. They were to show no mercy. Mordecai wanted the Jews to know and understand that the king was commissioning them "to gather and defend their lives, to destroy, to kill, and to annihilate any armed force of any people or province that might attack them, children and women included, and to plunder their goods" (Esther 8:11). All this Mordecai wrote in the name of King Ahasuerus and sealed the orders with the king's signet ring. After doing this, he sent the letters by couriers riding swift horses to spread the news throughout the land.

Then Mordecai dressed in the full regalia the king had given him and went out to announce to the people in Susa what had transpired. The Jews were filled with joy, but fear fell on the other citizens. Many declared themselves Jews because they were afraid. Now that it was apparent the king was backing the Jews, they were a force to be taken seriously. The power and influence of Mordecai increased, and so did the confidence of all the people. On the fateful day of the scheduled uprising, the few who dared to rise up against the Jews were squelched and destroyed, but the Jews laid no hand on the plunder. For them the victory was in knowing that God and the king were on their side, and they had been given authority to respond to their enemies.

~ellllee~

We know the Word of God stands. It cannot be reversed or revoked. Those who live submitted lives before Him know the power of walking in obedience to His instructions. A common saying is that "the Ten Commandments are not the ten suggestions." May I suggest that God's entire Word is to be taken seriously? It is the roadmap guaranteed to lead you to your best life. You can't do things your way and then ask God to bless your mess. He blesses us when we follow Him wholeheartedly.

One of the most overlooked facets of the Word is the authority of the believer—what the Word says about it and what it looks like in the life of every believer. The parallel between God the Father and King Ahasuerus in this story is stunning. Here we have a woman who is in trouble. She needs a redeemer to rescue her and her people from death. The king has allowed an advisor to write a mandate pretty much sealing the death of the Jews. But at the last minute, the king commands Mordecai to write a law that gives the Jews the opportunity to save themselves.

Today we are under a similar set of circumstances. The enemy has managed to get a writ of death against us through sheer manipulation way back in the Garden of Eden. We were doomed to die until God gave us the option through Jesus Christ to annihilate the power of the enemy in our lives. The more we submit to Christ, the greater power we have in His name. As we submit to God, the fear of God falls on our enemy, and he will flee from us just as the Word says in James 4:7.

How does this relate to a committed relationship or marriage? What does it look like? How are we going to apply this to our present set of principles? Simple. We're talking about "submission." Our favorite word as women, I'm sure. And yet it is where our power lies in the natural realm as well as the spiritual. In our study of Esther, we've seen that the theme of restraint is woven into the fiber of the story, along with submission and release. Esther kept submitting to the king and releasing him to make the final choice in how her enemy would be dealt with. In the end, because she allowed him to remain king in her interactions with him, he released her to be queen—and a safe queen at that. He released his authority to her. Now this is deep. Don't miss it! King Ahasuerus gave his queen the freedom to do as she pleased and gave his queen's closest relative the authority to rearrange one of his previous mandates. He gave Mordecai the authority on behalf of Esther.

But Mordecai had to use this authority. We can look at Mordecai as a parallel to the Holy Spirit in this story. Mordecai perpetuates the king's intentions on behalf of Esther and her people. Where the law had been put in place, he superimposed grace. It was grace that empowered the people to fight the good fight of faith against their enemies. It was grace that caused the fear of God to fall on their enemies and cause them to flee or to align themselves with the Jews.

My friend, if you can see the power of submission as an aggressive decision to put yourself in the position to be blessed by your king, your home will always be a haven and oasis from the storms of life. A husband who feels like a king in his home will always be willing to extend the grace of his authority to his wife. He won't make demands on her; he will free her to operate in her strengths. As a matter of fact, not only will he give her authority, but he will also equip her with everything she needs to exercise it. He won't be intimidated or frustrated by her power; instead, he will take delight in it and hold her up for all to see. He will celebrate her and bless her with his support and love like the husband in Proverbs 31 did for his wife, who was released by him to be a merchant, a farmer, a Realtor, and a mover and shaker in society. At the end of the day, he rose up and called her blessed. He celebrated her accomplishments.

Let us do away with the myth that men are intimidated by strong women. It's just not true. Now, I'm talking men, not boys. The problem comes when successful or strong women have problems releasing control. In actuality, a man is proud of a woman he can boast about, but he is not pleased when that woman won't allow him to be a man when he is with her.

I've watched a cousin and his wife balance this with such poetic beauty. Both are successful, strong people in their own right. But when people are with them, they'd never know what a heavyweight his wife is in international affairs. She honors and celebrates him and his gifts when they're together. And he is released to celebrate hers. He gives her the floor before his people, and she is treated like a queen. He admires her, and she has his ear. He doesn't feel threatened by her; he has his own sense of self. Although she's participated in mergers between countries and assisted presidents, she's not impressed with herself because her husband has slain his own dragons and prayed for presidents himself. They sing one another's accolades. They are confidantes and friends who have one another's backs. Together they are an unstoppable power couple.

If you want your man to give you power and authority in your home and your personal realms, you must first give it to your mate. And do it wholeheartedly because he will sense if it is an act. Know that when he releases you to wield the authority he gives you, that you need to use it for the benefit of both of you in securing your kingdom as a couple. The enemy should know your home is fortified territory he can't touch because you two are submitted to each other and to Jesus Christ.

Reflections

❈ How comfortable are you with the idea of submitting to your husband?

❈ In what ways does submission to your husband provide safety to you?

❈ When your husband isn't open to your ideas or requests, what is your usual response? In what ways can you inspire him to be more open to your suggestions?

Love Talk

One day a friend of mine asked her husband, "Honey, what makes you feel loved?" Her husband replied, "I feel loved when you do what I ask you to do." Shaunti Feldhahn wrote a book called *For Women Only*. She researched men. One of the questions she asked them was whether they would rather feel loved or respected. The majority voted for being respected! Small wonder God, through His Word, encourages women to submit, to walk in respect to their husbands.

In turn, their husbands will love them and give themselves for their wives as Christ loved and gave Himself for the church. One attitude begets another. The greatest way you can love your husband is to give him honor. As you do that, you will find that he will honor your word and your needs in ways you didn't dream possible. "Now to him who is able to do far more abundantly than all that we ask or think…" (Ephesians 3:20).

26

Unfinished Business

That very day the number of those killed in Susa the citadel was
reported to the king. And the king said to Queen Esther, "In
Susa the citadel the Jews have killed and destroyed 500 men
and also the ten sons of Haman. What then have they done in
the rest of the king's provinces! Now what is your wish? It shall
be granted you. And what further is your request? It shall be
fulfilled." And Esther said, "If it please the king, let the Jews who
are in Susa be allowed tomorrow also to do according to this day's
edict. And let the ten sons of Haman be hanged on the gallows."
So the king commanded this to be done. A decree was issued in
Susa, and the ten sons of Haman were hanged (Esther 9:11-14).

The reports kept coming in of what was taking place in the citadel of
Susa. Most citizens had chosen to side with the Jews to procure their
own safety. Those who had been poisoned by the propaganda against
the Jews chose to rise up against them and were met with miserable
defeat. The more the Jews struck down their enemies, the greater the
fear of them spread throughout the kingdom. Many who were against
the Jews withdrew before even engaging in the battle. In the end, the
Jews slew 500 people.

Then someone said, "What about Haman's sons? Will they continue his legacy of hatred?" On that note, the crowd turned and went

in search of Haman's 10 sons. The house of Haman had been given to Esther, so they weren't there. The friends who had gathered there to hear Haman's plots against Mordecai had scattered. This vengeance was exactly what they'd feared and predicted. They'd heard too much about the God of the Jews—that He didn't take kindly to His people being used or abused. They'd heard the stories of how the God of the Jews had delivered His people out of the hands of their enemies again and again. If this was the God Haman was contending against, he'd lost the battle before he even began the war. And now Haman's obsession had put them all in danger. At the news of his ironic end hanging from the gallows he'd had built for Mordecai, they had dispersed, keeping their distance from the rest of his family. They didn't want their association with Haman's family known.

Haman's sons were in hiding, but the Jews routed them out of their hiding places. Struck down without emotion, the 10 young men died for the sins of their father. After this last act was accomplished, a strange calm settled over the town of Susa. Each man went back to his home and wondered what would befall them on the morrow.

To assuage Esther's fears King Ahasuerus stood before her and gave her the report on what was happening. What did she want him to do next, he asked. Again he reassured her that whatever she wanted she could have, that her wish was his command.

Esther pensively considered what she'd been told. It sounded well and good, but she knew now wasn't the time to relax. She must finish what had been started to secure their peace and security in the days to come. If there were any residues of hatred and rebellion, it would surface in a matter of time. She wanted to make sure they didn't just stop at destroying the fruit but also took out any roots of the problem. The message had to be clear to all that anyone or anything that would come against the safety of her people wouldn't be tolerated.

She asked that tomorrow the Jews could do the same things they'd done today to route out any stragglers. She wanted the bodies of Haman's 10 sons to hang on the gallows as an example to anyone who might consider more violence against the Jewish people. She didn't want to come across as unfeeling, but she had to do whatever it took to make sure there wouldn't be a recurrence of this situation ever again. No, this circumstance would not be revisited. Neither would she let these events affect her marriage. She would make sure the matter was settled once and for all.

⁓ellഉⱳ⁓

There is temptation in every relationship when conflict arises. Some people try to smooth over the matter and then simply move on without dealing with the underlying issue. This doesn't lead to securing the health of any relationship. Usually in this situation, one or both partners fear confrontation. They don't like dealing with difficult matters or answering the hard questions that are necessary to address in order to resolve the issue. Yet the Word clearly states that the knowledge of the truth sets us free. The things that are never said often get us into trouble.

Sometimes things aren't said that need to be said because the participants don't really know what they want or need. This is dangerous because it begs the other partner to guess what the needs of the spouse are. This rarely works. I like the fact that King Ahasuerus was so direct with Esther. He stated what had been done to make sure he'd covered all the bases of what she'd previously asked for, and then he asked her what else he could do for her. He was ready to make her feel completely secure. This checking in is essential for both partners to do. That way they are clear about what has occurred between them, the effect of it, and what needs to be done to move past it. It is important to find out what the partner needs to feel good about the relationship and the future of it.

We women have a tendency to give our men what we think they need rather than what they say they want. If your man wants an apple, don't give him an orange and tell him it's better for him. Give him the apple! Learn to speak his language and convey love and service in ways that he understands.

When conflict arises, thrash it all the way out and leave no strings hanging. Settle the matter once and for all and refuse to revisit it. There is nothing worse than a partner or friend who stores up all the ills against you and then drags them out at the first opportunity after a perceived offense. There is nothing more disconcerting than trying to solve one conflict only to be reminded of 10 things you did wrong in the past. Those are seeds of bitterness that have taken root and affect the relationship in ways that come to light way after the fact.

Sometimes a partner in the relationship doesn't even realize why the ardor has cooled for his or her partner. The odds are that it's unresolved conflicts that were swept under the rug. Never dismiss a conflict because you're afraid to grab the bull by the horns, wrestle it to the ground, and slay it once and for all. People live together year after year while growing further and further apart because of the discussions they refuse to have. And it's not just the lack of discussions. There is also the lack of resolve to deal with the conflict. No conclusion was reached. No action steps taken so the offense wouldn't occur again.

We must slay the enemies in our midst instead of just cutting off their tails. It can and will grow another bigger and stronger tail! That means we must take the time to tackle the issues that cause problems in our relationships. Whether we seek counseling or do the work ourselves to come to a place of understanding, forgiveness, and new beginnings, it must be done.

Putting off resolving issues only leads to more problems as things fester and grow into a cancer that spreads and affects others beyond your personal relationship. Yes, your issues spread to others in your circle. As you share your feelings with others, they are driven to take sides, and on and on the conflict goes. Small wonder Proverbs tells us that a matter repeated separates friends (17:9). But when we are offended and hurt, it is hard to keep things to ourselves. Our pain is shed abroad, and others enter into our pain. Some add fuel to the fire, others discount our feelings, and still others try to help alleviate the situation. Usually after we've kissed and made up with our partners, the residue of the painful situation is still alive within our friends and other observers. They may struggle with forgiveness because they weren't part of the reconciliation process; therefore, they don't have the same ability to release the offense because of their allegiance to you.

There is no such thing as letting sleeping dogs lie in a relationship. What you keep inside will act out in negative ways that will affect your love for one another. You must get rid of anything that threatens the foundation and health of your relationship. Remember, it's the little foxes that ruin the vine (Song of Solomon 2:15). Nip anything in the bud that even looks like it may create a problem. That includes misunderstandings, lack of transparency, things said and unsaid, comments and questions raised by others that linger between you. Be fierce about letting nothing remain in your midst that might threaten your love for each other. This may mean some friends, activities, and habits may have to go. Some attitudes will have to be put to death. The priority isn't pleasing everyone; the priority is pleasing your spouse. When your partner feels that he is the priority above all else, he will move heaven and earth to make you feel loved.

Reflections

✣ How much do you internalize issues between your spouse and you? Why? What is the usual result of this?

✣ How does your partner respond when you bring up matters that bother you? What would it take to ease the resolution of your conflicts?

✣ When you let things go before an understanding was reached, what was the outcome? What can you do to get more positive results?

Love Talk

True love never skirts an issue or turns a blind eye away, no matter how painful the sight. Instead, it reviews the reality of the facts or offense and passionately seeks a solution to restore and cover the beloved. True love has the grace it takes to not concede to defeat or silence. Love confronts and puts to death anything that stands in its way in order to love more fully.

27

Celebration of Love

Therefore they called these days Purim...because of all that was written in this letter, and of what they had faced in this matter, and of what had happened to them, the Jews firmly obligated themselves and their offspring and all who joined them, that without fail they would keep these two days according to what was written and at the time appointed every year, that these days should be remembered and kept throughout every generation, in every clan, province, and city, and that these days of Purim should never fall into disuse among the Jews, nor should the commemoration of these days cease among their descendants. Then Queen Esther, the daughter of Abihail, and Mordecai the Jew gave full written authority, confirming this second letter about Purim...The command of Queen Esther confirmed these practices of Purim, and it was recorded in writing (Esther 9:26-29,32).

The sounds of celebration resounded around the city of Susa as the Jews feasted and celebrated the victory they had experienced over their enemies. On the second day of self-defense authorized by the king, the Jews killed another 300 men in Susa. Throughout the rest of the provinces, an additional 75,000 had fallen under the swords of the Jews. Now at last the Jewish people were free to give thanks to God for saving them. This was truly an occasion for a holiday!

Esther sat back, pondering all that had transpired in the last few days. The weight of it all finally sank in and overwhelmed her. She would have fainted if she didn't know the outcome. While it was happening, there had been no time for fear or any other distracting emotion, but now that the matter was concluded, she could feel her heart racing. Truly God had been faithful and delivered them from the snare of the enemy.

Mordecai was right. They should memorialize this time and observe it as a holiday every year lest they forget the great deliverance God had wrought for them. It was sadly true that those who forget the past are destined to repeat it. They also miss out on important lessons that can be learned. In this case, there was a major lesson that no one should forget: to walk uncompromisingly before God in faith is the way to honor. No matter how the enemy threatens or people are pressured, God takes care of His own when they follow His precepts and refuse to bow to any other god. No foe can stand undefeated in His presence. Yes, God had proven once again that He was their mighty God. Even the heathens acknowledged this was so.

Esther raised her hand, motioning the scribes to come forward. Let it be forever written and established that God had done great things for His people on this day. They'd been blessed, and they needed to always remember. Because they had been blessed, they should also bless one another on this day throughout the generations to come. It would be a ritual that even the children would honor. This time would be called Purim, and they would celebrate with feasting, joyous music, dance, and laughter. And they must give gifts to each other. It would be a time to acknowledge how precious life is and how great God is. It would remind them to never take a day or each other for granted. As they exchanged gifts and food, they would be reminded of the strength and importance of community.

Queen Esther learned she couldn't divorce herself from her people no matter how high the castle walls were. Neither did she want to. She appreciated her people in a whole new way. They were strong, resilient, and, most of all, God's. This entire situation was one more testament of the greatness of God and the power of family and community when people banded together for a common cause. She signed the Purim decree with a flourish. Yes, this was a moment in history that would stand for generations to come.

⁓⁓

There is a tendency in long-term relationships to forget things that should be remembered. When we memorialize the things God has brought us through, the bonds of friendship and marriage strengthen. Intimacy grows from surviving the trials of life. The testimony we gain from our experiences of mutual hardship makes our relationships stronger. Let's not be so quick to forget those times when we go through something together as couples. They make our union more powerful and lasting. The haste to forget the negative shouldn't make us throw out the baby with the bathwater. Remembering how we came through is the stuff that solidifies our love and passion for each other. The couple that doesn't go through any difficulties also doesn't experience the fullness of the redemptive nature of love.

The cedars of Lebanon were known as the strongest wood because they'd been broken by the wind. It is their brokenness and the sap that is spilled in the broken places that makes the wood so strong. Part of the process God uses to strengthen us is for us to be blessed, broken, and given to one another. Out of this brokenness comes new strength that makes our love more resilient. With every test and trial that we overcome, we should start a new celebratory ritual. One that helps us remember how God redeemed our relationships and made them into glorious reflections of His design for love.

Every couple should have rituals—times and specific things they do together to celebrate over and over again the days of their first love. We want to remember the good times as well as the struggles that have brought us this far. This helps us be more willing to forgive each other for any offenses or difficulties caused by the other. These celebrations help us refresh our love by doing the things we did together in the beginning that made us love each other in the first place. You know, what it took to get our partners is what it will take to keep our partners.

Familiarity makes people take one another for granted. There is a tendency to relax and not do what we used to do before. This sets the stage for the enemy to come in and do his dirty work. Let's say you always greeted your husband at the door perfectly coifed, smelling good, and looking even better for the first year you were married. But now he is lucky if you pull the rollers out of our hair and make it to the same room he is in. So he's wondering, *Where is the woman I married? I want that woman back!* Just because he gained a wife doesn't mean he doesn't still want the woman he courted. That's the woman he proposed to. The one who was always happy to see him and make him happy. That's the woman he still wants to see.

Sometimes after vows have been exchanged, people change. They believe their new roles require more somber models of who they were before. Not only do people change, but habits change as well as they settle into a more routine existence that does nothing to stoke passion. Perhaps a couple used to date before—go out to dinner, catch a movie, partake of an activity they both loved. Now all of that no longer occurs. It was these together moments that made both of you feel special and significant. You made time for one another. Just because you live together now doesn't mean this is no longer necessary. In fact, it is even more necessary! The rituals you create as a married couple not only renew your love for one another, but they become examples of what love looks like to the people around you, including your children. Your love and how you celebrate it can become a generational legacy.

One of my favorite memories of my parents was one morning when my dad had gotten into his car and driven down the street on his way to work. He got about a block before he turned around and came back. He parked the car and came inside the house. My mother looked up at him and asked if he'd forgotten something. He replied that he'd forgotten to kiss her! Imagine the impact that had on me as a preteen. I noted that when two people love each other, they never leave one another without acknowledging that love. My parents set the standard for what I looked for in a mate later in life. I want to carry on the legacy of their love in my own family. There were many things my parents did that made me feel secure as a child. I knew my parents loved one another. They put it on display before me. They made time for one another and had their own "stolen" moments where they were the first priority for each other. They were united. There would be no playing two ends against the middle with them. They were one. This was clearly apparent.

Your oneness is based on the things you do together to keep the enemy at bay. The devil will know he can't divide and conquer you because you have put things in place to keep your love fresh and your communication open. You are meeting each other's needs and creating new adventures between you that stir up passion. You have put rituals in place—a date night, a favorite activity, something that keeps you looking forward to spending time together—to promote your love. Remember, to the hungry soul every bitter thing seems sweet, but the full soul will loathe even the honeycomb (Proverbs 27:7). As you look to be there for your man, addressing his wants and needs and allowing him to be the man in your life, he will rise to new levels of what you've been looking for in him. As a matter of fact, may I dare say he will surprise you simply because you've given him room to be who he has been longing to be for you for a long time? While you've been longing for your man to be the king you've always dreamed of, he too has been dreaming of a queen resplendent in virtue and beauty.

A woman who inspires her man to rise to his best potential and lead his kingdom and household is truly a queen indeed.

Reflections

✄ In what ways do you memorialize the victories you share as a couple?

✄ What rituals have you put in place to refresh your love regularly?

✄ What can you do to renew your passion for your mate? What can you do to bring a sense of adventure to your relationship?

Love Talk

The influence a woman has on her man is above and beyond her imagination. She can make or break her man. In Africa there is this saying: "The man is the head, the woman is the neck. Wherever the neck turns the head turns." A profound little proverb! A woman's touch sets the tone or atmosphere in her home that lays the foundation for the response she will get from her man on any given issue. Anchor your relationship in moments and rituals that keep your man looking forward to being in your presence. This drive will inspire him to address your needs and please you by giving you his best self. As you celebrate him and all he does for you, he will search for new ways to be your king.

Final Thoughts

Mystery. Tension. Misunderstanding. Unspoken needs. Lack of communication. Passion. Lapses. Interferences. Every relationship has a myriad of ups and downs. We have to be able to take a deep breath and say to ourselves, "This is just a test. A test that our relationship must pass because every setback is a divine setup to take our love to the next level."

Our God is a God of process. He works to accomplish His will and do His good pleasure in our lives by redefining us through our experiences. He wants to finish the work He has begun in us, but He wants to do this with our cooperation. Sometimes in the midst of our relational issues we can't see where God is taking us, but we must trust Him and follow through to complete the process that takes us to a greater place of maturity.

One of my favorite Scriptures is found in Philippians. I love The Message version: "This is my prayer: that your love will flourish and that you will not only love much but well. Learn to love appropriately. You need to use your head and test your feelings so that your love is sincere and intelligent, not sentimental gush. Live a lover's life, circumspect and exemplary, a life Jesus will be proud of" (1:9). There it is. We can't afford to have a knee-jerk reaction every time something occurs in our relationships that we don't like. We must learn to process all of our emotions and responses through our God-filter that weeds out wrong thinking and attitudes so that we will respond the best way with our spouses or whomever we're dealing with in every situation.

The principles found in the story of Esther translate to how we relate to our spouses, our bosses, our best friends, our sisters, our brothers. They are universal principles that shouldn't be overlooked in the full circle of the story. It starts off with a queen who didn't realize her power or understand her position. Vashti was not submitted, and she reacted rather than responded to her man. She blew it, and she lost everything. We finish with Queen Esther, who didn't know her power, but she did know God's power. She responded rather than reacted to her king and husband. She understood her position and used it to her advantage. She submitted herself and her needs to her man and gained everything. What was the difference between the two women? One thought only of herself, and the other appealed to her husband for her needs by first appeasing his desires. This is the difference between the foolish woman who destroys her home with her own hands and the wise woman who builds her home and prepares a well-laid table (Proverbs 14:1; 9:2).

When dealing with your mate, it is always important to keep in mind his nature and needs. Only as you keep these things in perspective can you make quality decisions on how to respond in every circumstance. Keeping God as your marriage counselor on a daily basis guarantees that you'll get sound advice and a safe place to submit your disappointments and longings. As He takes them, He is able to deal with you and your spouse to bring you both to the place where your needs are met.

The bottom line in any relationship is that both people are really looking for the same things—to love and be loved. And not just loved but appreciated and made to feel significant. To want someone and be wanted by them is one of the most amazing feelings a person can ever experience. To know that person is willing to do anything for you to make you feel safe and loved is indescribable.

But the fact remains as well that love is not easy. It demands that you die to yourself countless times. True love goes against the grain of humanity. It is divine to love because it requires the fruit of the Spirit to love in a way that brings out the best in your beloved. To be patient when your needs are urgent requires a grace that only God can give. To consistently be kind when perhaps you don't feel kindness being returned is an exercise in rising above the flesh and remaining in the Holy Spirit. It is our nature to be possessive and to have an ego, yet real love is not jealous or boastful or proud or rude. There is selfishness in all of us, but if you truly love, you do not demand your own way. Yes, it is scary to release your own insistences because you literally have to surrender control. But that is love.

Love is not irritable or easily offended. The more pressure life applies to us, the more thin-skinned we become. And yet we must remember that this is an ungodly trait. Keeping no record of wrongs requires self-discipline. It is so easy to bring up everything someone did before to substantiate the present offense, yet that does more damage than anything else. There is no worse feeling than being unforgiven. Love forgives and releases without revisiting old offenses. Love rejoices when the truth wins out because the truth is liberating. Even if we don't like the truth, it is the medicine God sends to heal us after the initial sting.

Perhaps the most challenging aspect of love is it never gives up. Love is always hopeful and endures through every circumstance. That in itself should make us all push the pause button. In a world where most people enter relationships looking for what they can get without considering what they need to give, we need to change our focus to the joy of giving.

Loving well means loving as Christ loves. Selflessly, with no thought to or of Himself. Now some of you may be shaking your heads as you read this, wondering, "Is this really possible?" Yes, it is. But once again this requires asserting discipline. Disciplining your thoughts, attitudes, emotions, and actions. You will need to silence a lot of the voices you usually listen to because they're going to give you worldly advice that is contrary to what God says about your man and your situation. There is a way to do things in Christ that the world doesn't understand. The carnal mind doesn't comprehend the ways of the Holy Spirit. Though marriage is good to the flesh, the flesh still must be crucified to allow the Holy Spirit to reign in your relationship.

Truly marriage challenges you to pick up your cross and die daily more than ever. Love requires work to keep it healthy and alive. Marriage too is work. If you aren't willing to do the heart work, your relationship won't achieve the level God desires for you. Sometimes this means your emotions must be set aside for a time. You must use your head in some instances to preserve your relationship. If Christ had been ruled by His emotions, we might not have had a Savior. Can you imagine the outcome if He'd had a meltdown about the way people responded to Him and treated Him? We would all still be lost and dead in our sins. Instead, Jesus persevered. "For the joy that was set before him [Jesus] endured the cross, despising the shame" (Hebrews 12:2). Jesus forsook His human emotions and continued His plan to save us.

Why not consider the goals of your relationship? What do you want your relationship to look like? What outcome do you want? Then decide what steps you can take to get there. Esther systematically decided what her goal was, and then she developed a strategy for how she approached her husband for his help. I'm not proposing manipulation, but I am saying you need to exercise wisdom in your relationship. Don't grasp what you want at the expense of your mate; instead, empower your mate to meet your needs. In this way you both will be blessed.

At the end of the day, the way to get the best out of your man is to be your best for him and let him be your hero…your king.

Things to Remember

❋ Your home is a mini kingdom reflecting the relationship between God and man.

❋ When you treat your man like a king, he will treat you like a queen.

❋ What goes on at your house has an effect on your community and the kingdom of God.

❋ Your relationship is not a contest. It is a representation of divine teamwork. The team that plays together wins together.

❋ In adverse situations, consult with God *before* you react.

❋ Watch the company you keep. Don't listen to counsel that may damage your marriage.

❋ Never respond in the flesh; instead, pray and then get quiet and listen to what the Holy Spirit is saying.

❋ Make sure you've met the needs and reasonable wants of your man before you ask that he meet yours.

❋ Be clear about what your needs are, and then let your mate know. He doesn't have ESP.

❋ Your vulnerability empowers your mate to be your hero.

❋ "God [and men] opposes the proud, but gives grace to the humble" (Proverbs 3:34; James 4:6).

❋ Help your mate help you by giving him concrete ways he can meet your needs.

❋ Celebrate your partner when he gets it right.

❋ Create rituals in your relationship that will bring you back to your first love. Practice them often.

❋ Don't just love much, love well.

∾∿∿∾

To Contact Michelle,

find her on Facebook or Twitter, or
discover more about her ministry and books, log on to

www.MichelleHammond.com

∾∿∿∾

More Encouraging Books by
Michelle McKinney Hammond

101 Ways to Get and Keep His Attention
The DIVA Principle
How to Avoid the 10 Mistakes Single Women Make
How to Be Happy Where You Are
How to Be Found by the Man You've Been Looking For
How to Get Past Disappointment
The Power of Being a Woman
Right Attitudes for Right Living
Sassy, Single, and Satisfied
Secrets of an Irresistible Woman
What to Do Until Love Finds You
Why Do I Say "Yes" When I Need to Say "No"?
A Woman's Gotta Do What a Woman's Gotta Do

DVD
How to Get Past Disappointment (180 min.)

How to Get Past Disappointment
An Unforgettable Encounter

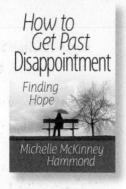

The Samaritan woman always welcomed the heat of the sun once she sat on the edge of the well and splashed her face with cool water from the bucket she drew up. This place was her oasis of peace and refreshing. But not today. A stranger was sitting in her spot. A Jewish rabbi...

Drawing on the dramatic story of the "Woman at the Well" found in John 4, bestselling author and dynamic speaker Michelle McKinney Hammond invites you to move beyond life's disappointments and experience God in a new and deeply fulfilling way. Through powerful, relevant biblical teaching, she encourages you to...

- let God's love help you face your hurts and forgive when necessary

- look beyond disappointment to embrace new beginnings

- release your expectations to discover even greater blessings in God's plan for you

As an added bonus, Michelle includes insightful questions and uplifting affirmations to help you live the life God wants you to have.

Also available
How to Get Past Disappointment DVD!
Let Michelle lead your group in six dynamic,
30-minute sessions.

Right Attitudes for Right Living
Attitude Is Everything!

Could your life use some positive reinforcement?

Are you looking for daily inspiration for your heart, mind, and spirit?

Do you want guidance in overcoming life's challenges or using your past experiences to transform your future?

Bestselling author and dynamic speaker Michelle McKinney Hammond knows that making the best life choices isn't always easy. With understanding, compassion, and biblical wisdom, she offers fresh perspectives, motivating affirmations, and get-it-done suggestions to encourage you to get the most from life. You can...

※ make wise choices

※ life joyfully

※ transform your life

※ master your circumstances

HARVEST HOUSE PUBLISHERS
EUGENE, OREGON

To learn more about books by Michelle McKinney Hammond
and to read sample chapters, log on to:
www.HarvestHousePublishers.com